Practical, inspirational, and action-packed, Jay's book gives us a clear road map for living with intention, purpose, and joy. I can hardly wait to see my relationships deepen—with God, those around me, and even myself—as I put these incredible ideas into action!

Michelle Watson
author of *Dad, Here's What I Really Need from You*

Jay Payleitner has done it again with *What If God Wrote Your To-Do List?* The content is sometimes silly, sometimes serious—which helps us to let our guard down so God can work in us. I also appreciate the brevity of each chapter, which allows me to read one and then have time to reflect on what I just read and make an application. This book is insanely simple and practical, yet it's substantial enough to help us become more like Christ.

Tom Cheshire
founder, Relevant Practical Ministry for Men

Words cannot express how important this book is. It is practical yet deep, entertaining yet instructive. Some passages will help you survive, and some will empower you to thrive.

Carey Casey
president, National Center for Fathering

Reading Jay's newest book, I felt lightened, not loaded down. No guilt here—but plenty of gold! Simple. Profound. Spot-on. Once again, Jay has helped us set our minds on things above. I want God to write my to-do list!

Jon Gauger
Moody Radio host and author of *If I Could Do It All Over Again*

WHAT IF
GOD
WROTE YOUR
TO-DO
LIST?

JAY PAYLEITNER

HARVEST HOUSE PUBLISHERS
EUGENE, OREGON

Cover design by Bryce Williamson

Cover Image © -Panya-, Naphat_Jorjee / iStock

Published in association with The Steve Laube Agency, LLC, 24 W. Camelback Rd. A-635, Phoenix, Arizona 85013.

To Judah, Jackson, Emerson, Gideon, Reese, and Nolan

WHAT IF GOD WROTE YOUR TO-DO LIST?

Copyright © 2018 Jay Payleitner
Published by Harvest House Publishers
Eugene, Oregon 97408
www.harvesthousepublishers.com

ISBN 978-0-7369-6193-6 (pbk.)
ISBN 978-0-7369-6194-3 (eBook)

Library of Congress Cataloging-in-Publication Data

Names: Payleitner, Jay K., author.
Title: What if God wrote your to-do list? / Jay Payleitner.
Description: Eugene : Harvest House Publishers, 2018.
Identifiers: LCCN 2017035179 (print) | LCCN 2017055269 (ebook) | ISBN 9780736961943 (ebook) | ISBN 9780736961936 (pbk.)
Subjects: LCSH: Christian life—Miscellanea. | Spiritual life—Miscellanea. | Lists.
Classification: LCC BV4501.3 (ebook) | LCC BV4501.3 .P3985 2018 (print) | DDC 248.4—dc23
LC record available at https://lccn.loc.gov/2017035179

Printed in the United States of America

19 20 21 22 23 24 25 26 / BP-SK / 10 9 8 7

Contents

Foreword

by Josh D. McDowell

Is it possible that God has a to-do list for each and every one of us? Certainly!

Several familiar verses in the Bible confirm that we all have unique gifts (Romans 12:6). And we can know what God expects of us, because we are able to "test and approve what God's will is" (Romans 12:2).

What's more, we can walk in confidence that God's plan is carefully crafted and extraordinary. "We are God's masterpiece. He has created us anew in Christ Jesus, so we can do the good things he planned for us long ago" (Ephesians 2:10 NLT).

Still, before you start scrambling to check off items on your personalized to-do list from God, allow me to confirm that you cannot work your way into heaven. "For it is by grace you have been saved, through faith—and this not from yourselves, it is the gift of God—not by works, so that no one can boast" (Ephesians 2:8-9). Grace is the unmerited favor of a loving God, wholly demonstrated in the sacrifice of his Son.

We should also remember that the omnipotent Creator of the universe doesn't really need our help. He's quite capable of keeping the world spinning without you or me. And yet he invites us to be invested and involved in his plan *for our own sake.* Tackling God's to-do list for our lives reveals how God works. We see the power of unconditional love. We see how love wins, truth matters, and justice ultimately prevails. By raising our hand and saying, "Here I am, Lord, send me," our faith and convictions grow. We learn to trust and surrender every aspect of our lives. We experience the privilege of being used by God.

Without a doubt, God wants us to take action. The entire book of James emphasizes the importance and value of work. James 2:17 says, "Faith by itself, if not accompanied by action, is dead." Looking back at more than 50 years of ministry, that biblical idea—along with the Holy Spirit's prompting—is what led me to write more than 100 books, travel to more than 100 countries, and speak to more than 25 million people.

Don't worry! Each individual is unique. Your to-do list looks a lot different from mine. But don't be surprised if God's plan for your life takes you to unexpected places to do revolutionary things. On the other hand, there are things you can check off your to-do list this very day without leaving your corner of the world.

That simple idea might be the biggest takeaway from this book. There are things you can do in the next *two minutes* to make a difference in the life of another person. In the next *two days,* you can uncover an old truth, share a fresh perspective, right a wrong, or turn over a new leaf. In the next *two weeks,* you could host a rally, rethink your career, or recruit an army.

As you ease your way through this book, please don't treat the contents page like a checklist. No one expects you to check or circle every item. But I believe you will find something in these 52 chapters to inspire you to action sooner than you may imagine.

Along the way, be careful, be wise, and take full advantage of every opportunity. As Paul writes in Ephesians 5:15-17, "Be very careful, then, how you live—not as unwise but as wise, making the most of every opportunity, because the days are evil. Therefore do not be foolish, but understand what the Lord's will is."

You Already Have Plenty of Things to Do

I know. Your to-do list gets longer every day.

Change your oil. See the dentist. Back up your computer. Change the furnace filter. Book a hotel room for that out-of-town wedding. Renegotiate your student loan. Clean out your desk. Clean out the fridge. Get your passport. Download those photos. Renew your library card. Replace your toothbrush. Test the smoke alarms. Update your CV. Etcetera.

Good news. None of those things are in this book. Because those are things that go on *your* to-do list.

This book describes things you can do today, tomorrow, or this week that might be on *God's* to-do list. That includes things that nudge you (or inspire you) to live more in line with God's plan for your life. Things that matter. Things that lead to less stress and more joy. Things that lead to achievements and triumphs you never thought possible. Some of these ideas have been on your radar for a while. Some will be total surprises.

FYI: This book is a sequel to *What If God Wrote Your Bucket List?* While that bestseller delivers things to do before you kick the bucket, this book imagines valuable strategies that have a little more urgency. Stuff to consider first thing in the morning, before the sun sets, or sometime in the next week or so.

My suggestion is, don't neglect your own to-do list. You *should* have a passport and library card. Take care of your teeth. That fuzzy lump in the back of the refrigerator needs to get tossed. But that's all routine maintenance.

You were designed, created, and placed on this earth for so much more. What you really want to do is stuff that leads to greatness. That's what you'll find on God's to-do list for your very near future.

Congratulations on joining this journey. You will not be sorry.

*We can get so wrapped up in the grind of daily life that we
forget life is a gift to be unwrapped each and every day.*

Jay Payleitner

Make Your Bed

Is this controversial? Perhaps. *When, who, how,* and *why* seem to be legitimate concerns in some homes regarding the topic of making the bed.

I am not a bed-making expert, and I assume neither are you. Still, I believe we can come to reasonable conclusions on these four one-word questions.

The question of *when* is easy. Do it soon after waking up. Perhaps immediately, as soon as your feet hit the floor. Or within minutes after your shower. Once you pour your coffee or grab breakfast, your day has begun. At that point, you want any bedmaking duties behind you.

The question of *who* may be tricky, but it needn't be. Because I speak at marriage conferences, I have learned that "who makes the bed" is quite often a point of conflict and dispute. Some guys actually think it is "woman's work." I've actually heard men shout that from the audience. (Yikes.) Wives sometimes put "making the bed" on the list of household chores to be divided equally and meticulously. Keeping score on minor housekeeping duties is a formula for finger-pointing and rancor. There's a better way.

Let me put that *who* question to rest forever. The answer is "who-ever gets up last!" If an early rising spouse does choose to circle back and make the bed, that gesture should be considered a gift, and a sincere "thanks for making the bed" would be quite appropriate.

If it's your own bed, the *how* is totally up to you. But for married couples, it can also be a point of conflict. She might have a half dozen throw pillows that need to be arranged just so. He doesn't do that very well. On the other hand, he might have a preferred method of sheet and comforter tucking and smoothing that she doesn't do exactly right. I recommend that whoever does the bed making gets to decide on the *how*.

Which brings us to the question of *why?* Which is the real point of this chapter. And perhaps the real point of this book.

You may be asking, why even get out of bed in the morning? How do you start your day in a way that leads to completing relevant tasks? What's the strategy for hitting your pillow at night with a satisfaction that life is not just passing you by?

First, you need to get out of bed so you can fulfill the plan God has for your life. You may not know what it is, but you won't find it laying down on the job. "We are God's masterpiece. He has created us anew in Christ Jesus, so we can do the good things he planned for us long ago" (Ephesians 2:10 NLT). In other words, at some point you have to stop dreaming and start doing. Once your bed is made, you are less likely to jump back in.

Second, making your bed begins your day with an achievement. US Navy Admiral William H. McRaven, the commander of the US Special Operations Command who oversaw the raid to capture or kill Osama bin Laden, included this in his remarks to the graduates of his alma mater:

> Make your bed every morning…It will give you a small sense of pride, and it will encourage you to do another task, and another, and another. And by the end of the day that one task completed will have turned into many tasks completed. Making your bed will also reinforce the fact that the little things in life matter. If you can't do the little things right, you'll never be able to do the big things right.

And if by chance you have a miserable day, you will come home to a bed that is made—that you made—and a made bed gives you encouragement that tomorrow will be better.

If you want to change the world, start off by making your bed.

Third, mundane activities often lead to great rewards. Making your bed, sweeping your porch, or doing routine filing on the job may seem inconsequential. But it all matters. People notice. Small tasks done well lead to greater responsibilities. Turning chaos to order sharpens the mind and makes progress possible. By paying attention to detail, you'll notice something of vital importance that others might overlook.

You really never know what activities will matter most. On any given day, what you do *now* could have a much greater impact on the world than what you do *later*. Ecclesiastes 11:6 confirms, "Sow your seed in the morning, and at evening let your hands not be idle, for you do not know which will succeed, whether this or that, or whether both will do equally well."

So are you convinced? Is "make your bed" now at the top of your daily to-do list? Don't worry—that's not a requirement for turning the page. After all, there are 51 more items you'll want to consider.

Checking the List

Making your bed in the morning is a specific task. And it's a metaphor. If you begin your day, week, or year with a small achievement, bigger achievements are more likely to follow.

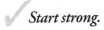 *Start strong.*

Eat the Frog

Ya gotta love the quote, "Eat a live frog first thing in the morning and nothing worse will happen to you the rest of the day." The quotation is often attributed to Mark Twain, but was most likely first spoken by the eighteenth century French playwright and street orator Nicolas Chamfort.

So what does it mean? Well, Chamfort certainly wasn't suggesting we should keep a supply of carnivorous, tailless amphibians in the fridge to munch on before our Cheerios.

One interpretation is that eating a live frog for breakfast is a strategy for making sure you have a productive day. What's worse than looking back at a perfectly good day and realizing that you haven't done squat? Sure, once in a while you need to take a vacation day. But most days you want to do something big. Eating a frog may not seem worthwhile or valuable, but you have to admit, it's not a small task.

Early morning frog feasting may also be a pretty good strategy when faced with a long list of things to do. Tackle the most challenging project first. When that initial huge burden is complete, suddenly the rest of your chores don't seem so onerous.

Maybe it was Chamfort's tactic for overcoming procrastination. If you've been dragging your feet and delaying a project, it may be a good idea to bounce out of bed tomorrow morning, hold your nose, and finally swallow that frog.

I can't imagine Nicolas Chamfort or Mark Twain heading off to Gold's Gym or Planet Fitness. I doubt they had a personal trainer or went to a daily Pilates class. But I know I would probably feel healthier, stronger, and wiser if I got up every morning and sweat for an hour or so. It's not going to happen though. For me, that sounds about as attractive as eating a live frog.

With that in mind, maybe a daily workout is my designated edible frog. Which leads to the question, what's yours? What frog should you eat sooner rather than later? It doesn't have to be something disgusting. It's just something you can do every morning or in the next few hours that will significantly improve the rest of your day or week.

Getting exercise is obvious. Walking around the block. Spending fifteen minutes on the treadmill or elliptical. A few sun stretches and downward dogs to loosen your muscles and get your blood flowing.

Spending twenty minutes to clear your inbox and briefly check social media, and then closing down those distractions until after lunch might be an expeditious way to start the day. Or maybe don't even peek at a screen at all until after lunch. Is that something you can do? Wouldn't limiting your access to technology make you more productive?

If you're typically still in your jammies at noon, then showering, teeth brushing, and dressing might be your frog.

If your morning commute finds you arriving on the job bleary-eyed and nonproductive, then maybe you need to start your day with a light, healthy breakfast. (Getting to bed a bit earlier might also be a good idea.)

It's a far cry from actually eating a frog, but a regular meeting with an accountability partner would help you reboot your entire outlook on life. Being open and honest once a week with a trusted accomplice will help you filter out the crud in your life and commit to pursuing truth, beauty, and grace.

Finally—and this will come as no surprise—the most beneficial choice you can make every morning is to read a chapter or two from Scripture and journal your discoveries. That habit would actually be the opposite of eating a frog. As a matter of fact, Psalm 119:103 (NASB) promises, "How sweet are Your words to my taste! Yes, sweeter than honey to my mouth!"

All that to say, despite Mr. Chamfort's recommendation, taking a moment each morning to submit to the Lord and ask for his guidance and mercies is actually much more effective than any frog breakfast. It may take a bit of personal discipline. But indulging in God's Word is a perfectly delicious and satisfying way to start your day.

Checking the List

Eating a frog (figuratively speaking) takes courage and discipline. But the rewards are many. Hebrews 12:11 (ESV) promises, "For the moment all discipline seems painful rather than pleasant, but later it yields the peaceful fruit of righteousness to those who have been trained by it."

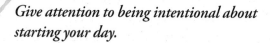 *Give attention to being intentional about starting your day.*

Read Something
Longer Than a Tweet

Every morning, I saunter down to the end of my driveway to pick up two newspapers. The *Chicago Tribune* and the *Daily Herald*. As I look up and down my street, I can't help but notice that only one other driveway has any newspaper at all. And it makes me sad.

I think about all my neighbors who miss the satisfaction of seeing what's going on in the world at a pace they control. They are missing out on the joy of scanning headlines and digging deeper into topics they had not anticipated exploring this day. Or ever.

News. Business. Sports. Lifestyle. Entertainment. Comics. Editorial. Every day I spread out those pages on my kitchen table and discover stuff that has me shaking my head, thinking new thoughts, checking my calendar, and laughing right out loud. I share something with Rita. I share something with the world.

Of course, I disagree with some of the editorial writers. Also, the one-sided spin on some of the supposed straight news stories is painfully obvious. But even that makes me wiser, sharper, and better prepared to argue on the side of truth. Part of me wishes everyone still got a newspaper and spent a half hour with it every day. I think we might all better understand each other.

Before jumping to too many conclusions, it's possible that I'm reading the situation all wrong. There are actually more effective methods of disseminating the same kinds of information. We all know printed newspapers are out of date. Subscription rates are plummeting. And quite literally the news is at least eight hours old by the time it reaches my driveway. Honestly, the computer screens sitting on just about every desk in the country are better conduits for news.

It's entirely possible my neighbors—and yours—spend extended thoughtful time reading long articles online about a wide variety of subjects. I know I can't, but maybe they can maintain focus on a single topic for several minutes at a time, ignoring the pop-up ads for weight loss products and asthma cures. Somehow those people have reinforced their resistance and don't feel the need to click on links that warn about identity theft and computer viruses or promise "jaw-dropping photos."

The great fear, of course, is that most people get their news in tweet-sized bites or listen only to media outlets with whom they already agree. Plus, online news comes so fast and furious that we have zero time to absorb or contemplate what we just read, saw, or heard. Even worse, we pass it on or add comments without checking the source or considering how it measures up to biblical truth.

Philippians 4:8 reminds us that what we think about matters. "Finally, brothers and sisters, whatever is true, whatever is noble, whatever is right, whatever is pure, whatever is lovely, whatever is admirable—if anything is excellent or praiseworthy—think about such things."

The art of thinking requires humans to string together bits of memory, knowledge, advice, experience, and dreams. You can't do that in a 140-character tweet or a one-second GIF. You can't do that if a new high-def image flashes across your field of vision every three seconds. You can't do that without taking in significant chunks of new information and allowing them to roll around in your skull for several minutes, hours, or days.

The first-century Greek philosopher Epictetus said, "No great thing is created suddenly." We might add this thought: "Great ideas may come in a brilliant flash of inspiration, but only after gathering enough kindling, accelerant, and friction to create the spark."

Checking the List

Is thinking on your to-do list? It should be. And the strategy for being productively thoughtful is to dwell long and hard on ideas that uplift rather than drag down. Maybe start with Colossians 3:2: "Set your minds on things above, not on earthly things."

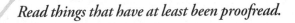 *Read things that have at least been proofread.*

Accept the Second Chance

You will mess up this week. It's inevitable. On the job. At school. In a hastily written tweet or post. With your spouse, kids, parents, or BFF. Possibly talking with a store clerk, a phone solicitor, or a traffic cop. Maybe the impact is deeply troublesome. Maybe it was a small thing. Maybe no one notices your mistake except you.

When you realize you messed up, you have two choices. You can admit it, make things right, and take steps so it doesn't happen again. Or you can do the opposite. Deny it, make excuses, blame someone else, get angry, or hide the evidence, hoping no one ever finds out about it.

You know what you need to do. And so did Cain. You remember his story from the very first pages of your Bible. But you probably don't remember that God gave him a *second chance*, and his unfortunate response took the situation from bad to worse.

In Genesis, we read about Cain and his brother making offerings to God. Sounds like a good idea, right? Except when Cain offered his gifts to the Lord, they were rejected, leaving Cain ticked off. What made it even more irritating was that God seemed to be delighted with the gift from his little brother, Abel. The Bible doesn't say specifically why Cain's gift wasn't worthy. But we get a hint when we read that Abel's gift was top-notch—the best of the firstborn lambs from his flock. Maybe

Cain skimped, not giving God his best. Maybe his heart just wasn't in the right place.

In any case, God still gave Cain a second chance and even spelled out the consequences if he didn't do what was right. "You will be accepted if you do what is right. But if you refuse to do what is right, then watch out! Sin is crouching at the door, eager to control you. But you must subdue it and be its master" (Genesis 4:7 NLT).

What does Cain do with his second chance? Does he gratefully fill a bushel basket with his finest vegetables and offer them to God? Does he ask Abel for help in preparing a sweeter offering? You know what happens. He ignores the instruction, commits the first murder, loses the ability to grow crops, and is banished to wander the earth away from the presence of the Lord.

Cain was given a second chance. But he chose to dig a deeper hole, and he paid a steep price. Cain's story is the perfect illustration of the promise found in Proverbs 28:13: "People who conceal their sins will not prosper, but if they confess and turn from them, they will receive mercy" (NLT).

For sure, God is love. But God is also *just*. He has given us plenty of ways to know right from wrong. Even when we make a wrong choice, he will often give us ample opportunity to turn back to him. But in the end, he leaves it up to us.

So here's the next item on your to-do list. Later this week, don't ignore the Holy Spirit when he says, "Make that apology," "Take back your little white lie," or "Flee that impure thought." That's your second chance. Take it. You may not get another.

Checking the List

God speaks directly to Cain and gives some pretty clear instruction. He says, "Do what is right." That tells us a few things worth remembering: There is a right and wrong. We can know it. We have a choice. We need to follow the path of righteousness because there are consequences if we don't! Thankfully, we're not alone in this fight. Genesis 4:7 also tells us, although sin is waiting to pounce, God has provided a way to face sin and claim victory.

 When God offers a way out, take it.

Go Back to High School

Remember high school? Would you describe your experience as good times, not-so-good times, bleak times, or fast times? Were you relieved when those four (or five) years were over? Or maybe you peaked in high school, and your yearbook is filled with joyous memories.

Some people experience waves of regret when their high school days come to mind. Regretting things they did. Regretting things they didn't do. If they could go back, most people say they would change a few things. A study by Netscape Internet Service found that 63 percent of US adults said if they could redo their high school years, they would think ahead about the future and college. Sixty-one percent said they would study harder and get better grades.

This item on your to-do list has nothing to do with regrets, but everything to do with taking advantage of a resource that is not far from your home. Set aside any emotions from your teenage years and head over to your local high school for a sporting event, choir concert, art show, or theatre production.

The benefits overflow. For one, you're investing in your hometown. In small-town Texas, where football is king, most of the residents show up for Friday Night Lights. Even in big cities, local crowds come out to support the young artists and athletes cultivating their new skills.

Watching those fresh faces filled with determination and spirit imparts a ray of hope for the future. Surrounding yourself with proud moms and dads, students, and neighbors reminds you that you're part of a community.

In addition, that auditorium, gymnasium, or stadium is a treasure of like-minded people. Maybe even a new friend or two. Everyone is there to support the students. Some of my most cherished relationships were formed attending my own kids' high school activities. Standing in line at the concession stand, it's easy to strike up a conversation with a stranger. "Pretty good game, huh?"

As an adult, setting foot on a high school campus helps you put your own four years of high emotion into context. Styles change, curriculum evolves, and technology zooms ahead. But sixteen-year-old kids are still sixteen-year-old kids. They face an uncertain future. They're trying to fit in. Broken hearts, acne, cliques, stressing out about grades, slamming lockers, swarming hallways, finding a prom date, and facing peer pressure will always be parts of the high school experience.

It's not a bad thing to consider what things you might have done differently, but this could also be your wake-up call. Take a close look at those kids on that stage or playing field. At this season of their young lives, those young people truly believe they are enduring a life-or-death experience. One dropped pass, one missed note, one snub from the popular girl, or one C-minus signals the end of the world. But you know it's not.

You are well aware that decisions and experiences *after* high school have much greater significance. Also, because you can look back, you know there's a future for those kids beyond high school. And—listen carefully—there's a future for you beyond today.

It doesn't matter whether you were a jock, cheerleader, brainiac, rebel, loner, artist, or class clown. That was then. Visiting a high school campus as an adult, you may find yourself shaking your head as you consider how much significance you assigned to so many of your decisions, victories, or failures. Yes, high school is a big deal. We all carry part of our teenage self with us. But it doesn't have to define our entire lives.

The question is not, what do you regret from high school? The question is, what will you do from here?

Checking the List

We don't want to live in the past. Or dwell on the past. Or run from the past. But we can *reflect* on the past to help us see that God can make all things new. The prophet Isaiah wrote, "Forget the former things; do not dwell on the past. See, I am doing a new thing! Now it springs up; do you not perceive it? I am making a way in the wilderness and streams in the wasteland" (43:18-19).

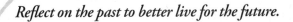 *Reflect on the past to better live for the future.*

Shine

J esus begins his ministry by getting baptized by John, allowing himself to be tempted in the desert by Satan for forty days, recruiting some fishermen, and then teaching in synagogues, preaching the good news, and healing all varieties of diseases and sickness.

Not surprisingly, word spreads. When the crowds increase, he finds a nice comfy corner of a mountainside—probably with excellent acoustics—and delivers perhaps the most amazing speech of all time. We've come to call it the Sermon on the Mount. It begins with the Beatitudes, found in Matthew 5.

Right away, Jesus makes it clear that he has come to turn the world upside down. He talks about the meek inheriting the earth. He provides a strategy for seeing God. Many of those in attendance may have been surprised to hear that it's not about who you know or how much power you have. It's about having a pure heart. The Beatitudes also specify that people who are blessed the most all seem to have some kind of need. They're hungry, thirsty, mourning, or persecuted.

Next we find a couple of well-known metaphors. Jesus tells all those listening, "You are the salt of the earth," and "You are the light of the world." To those tracking with Jesus, that makes sense. Salt preserves food and enhances flavor. Light, of course, helps people know the way.

Providing nourishment, enrichment, and direction for the soul are worthwhile attributes.

Then comes Matthew 5:16: "Let your light shine before men in such a way that they may see your good works, and glorify your Father who is in heaven" (NASB).

As far as I can see, this is the first recorded *instruction* from Jesus to a crowd. Grammarians would call it an imperative. And you know what? This verse just might be a formula for life, our reason for living on this planet. We are called to live and act in such a way that people look at us and say, "He makes the world a better place," or "She brings joy to everyone she meets." But we can't stop there. We need to identify ourselves as Christians so God gets the credit for our good works.

If we do good works without acknowledging whom we serve, then we get the glory ourselves. That's not a good plan. That glory should go to God.

What does that look like? On the job, be known as someone who always tells the truth, gives credit where credit is due, respects authority, and would never pad an expense account. In your neighborhood, keep your lawn mowed and your sidewalk swept. Greet neighbors with a smile, help carry in their groceries, and bring over some chicken soup, fresh-cut flowers, or a plate of Christmas cookies as life unfolds. Around your community, build a reputation as a problem solver and voice of reason rather than someone who whines, gossips, or spends more time talking than listening.

Be the kind of person others seek out when they have a problem because you seem to have wisdom that comes from beyond our world. Apologize when you mess up. Deal with adversity with patience and grace. Let the fruit of the Spirit (Galatians 5:22-23) show up in your life. And here's an idea—when you ask, "How are you?" actually mean it and listen for the answer.

In other words, be a follower of Christ. But don't stop there.

Once you've established yourself as a true-blue straight shooter with an auspicious track record, make sure your colleagues, neighbors, friends, and acquaintances know the source of your good works. Don't hide your faith. Without being bombastic, establish a reputation as a follower of Christ. Maybe have a single tasteful plaque with a relevant passage of Scripture in your office. Be seen reading your Bible at lunch. Sprinkle your conversation with an occasional biblical affirmation. When appropriate, mention a good story or insight you heard at church over the weekend. Give a good review to a movie or book with a theme of faithfulness or restoration. If the conversation opens the door to a spiritual discussion or invitation, be gentle and respectful. When witnessing repercussions of our fallen world, offer less judgment and more grace. When someone comes to you for advice because they're going through a tough time—and they will—share a scriptural truth and promise your prayers. Maybe pray with them in the moment.

Colossians 4:5-6 delivers some thoughtful guidance when it comes to those interactions. Again, the goal is to be salty—in a good way. "Be wise in the way you act toward outsiders; make the most of every opportunity. Let your conversation be always full of grace, seasoned with salt, so that you may know how to answer everyone."

The goal in all of this is to reflect Jesus and glorify our Father in heaven. To be *winsome* so that you might "win some" for Christ. The methodology might be summed up in one word—"shine."

Checking the List

Make the world wonder what got into you. And then tell 'em.

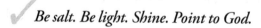 *Be salt. Be light. Shine. Point to God.*

Pause Before Posting

There are quite a few reasons to spend less time viewing screens. Distracted driving leads to car wrecks. Distracted walking leads to pedestrians falling off curbs, smacking into signs, tripping over hydrants, and splashing into courtyard fountains. Texting at the dinner table irritates dining partners. Answering emails in a conference room when your boss is speaking may get you fired. Watching three hours of reality shows, hospital dramas, political commentary, or other television programming every night adds up to more than a thousand hours out of your life every year you can never get back.

But perhaps the most dangerous use of a screen is receiving and delivering interactive social media faster than the speed of thought. Click on a social network, and you are instantly slammed with images and ideas that provoke you to respond without fully engaging your common sense and considering all the ramifications.

Admit it. More than once you've fired off a response on Facebook, Instagram, LinkedIn, or some other social media site that you wish you could take back. Or worse, maybe you've clicked Send and never realized how much damage or pain you caused with your post.

Here are a few examples of why you need to include "Pause before posting" on your to-do list.

Damaging the reputation of a friend. You and your pal have all kinds of inside jokes. And they're mostly harmless. You've known each other a long time, and you know he or she really isn't a hater or a criminal. But when you forward something meant for your eyes only, you could be opening your friend up to some judgment or ridicule. Of course, maybe they shouldn't have sent that post to begin with.

Damaging the reputation of your pastor or church. You love your church. You've invested emotionally, spiritually, and financially in the people and programs. Which gives you the right to express a concern about something that doesn't feel right. That may include a theological issue, a stewardship concern, or even a complaint about the music, stage lights, parking lot, new building project, and so on. I urge you to share the concern only with your small group and church leadership. If you rant online, only bad things happen. And you can't take it back.

Giving too much information. Maybe you are brokenhearted about a concern shared in confidence by a friend or acquaintance. Maybe some neighborhood news has hit you hard, and you're seeking prayer partners to bring that crisis before the throne of God. Well, it may not be your job to reveal personal information about a struggling marriage, personal difficulty, grim diagnosis, or a teenager who's going off the deep end. There's a reason they call it TMI.

Taking a stand. You can go there if you want. But you need to understand that very rarely will your snide comment or your reposting of someone else's snide comment ever change anyone's opinion. Yes, there are loads of short videos—some well-produced and some rather embarrassing—that speak to your heart. If you share them, half your audience will cheer, and half your audience will shake their heads. Again, feel free to go there. But you might want to pause momentarily to consider whether that is where you really want to be.

Showing off. This may be a gray area. Your friends want to celebrate your victories and successes. Go ahead and send that pic of your toes extended out toward the beach. Share a selfie with your sweetie at Cinderella's castle. A full stringer of walleye and perch. Graduation day. Your ridiculously cute grandkids. But please remember, when it comes to posting self-indulgent photos, less is more. Especially since some of your online friends can't afford a vacation, don't have a sweetie, or never see their grandkids for whatever reason. And even if someone "likes" your post, that doesn't mean they like your post.

In addition, it's worth reminding ourselves that there is no such thing as a private posting on social media. Even Snapchat posts—which supposedly disappear in a matter of seconds—can be saved, retrieved, or grabbed via easily obtainable apps.

The last word on this topic comes from a recent public service campaign aimed at students, which has some value for grownups as well. *Think* before you send, share, or forward a social media post. That's T-H-I-N-K. As in, ask yourself five questions before you dispatch that posting with your name on it forever into the world. Is it true? Is it helpful? Is it inspiring? Is it necessary? Is it kind? Good advice for kids and adults.

Checking the List

Sometimes our to-do list includes stuff we actually need *not* to do. Or stuff we need to be more careful about. In our fast-paced world, we tend to hurry and do stuff that we may have reconsidered if we had just slowed down for a moment.

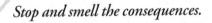 *Stop and smell the consequences.*

Notice Squirrels, Armadillos, and Kangaroos

I rarely notice squirrels. When they climb my wife's birdfeeder and scatter sunflower seeds all over the corner of our patio, I curse them mildly. But if I see one perched on a tree branch, I certainly don't squeal with amazement, "Look—a squirrel!" That's because here in the Midwest, they're everywhere.

On the other hand, when a business trip took me to south Texas, I slammed on my brakes to marvel at an armadillo waddling along the roadside. Thankfully, my host in the passenger seat was wearing his seatbelt. He laughed a bit before saying, "Really? You almost killed us for an armadillo? We'll probably see five more in the next two miles."

I've not visited Australia. (It's on my bucket list.) But I understand that once you get out of the cities, kangaroos are more of a nuisance than an attraction. They frequently tend to make life difficult for drivers, farmers, and golfers. If a kangaroo leaped across your path in North America, you'd tell that story for the rest of your life. In Australia, not so much.

The lesson seems to be that we take for granted the things we see every day. That's not surprising because…well, we see them every day. We lose appreciation for things that are familiar, like local wildlife, the ability to tie your shoes, a full cupboard, photographs, windows, our five senses, or the seasons.

But wait a second! Those things actually are quite astounding. Have you ever really watched a squirrel climb *down* a tree or jump from one little branch to another little branch? Incredible.

And how is it possible for you to tie your shoelaces without thinking about it? *Loop, swirl, push through, grab, snap.* But you do it!

Plus, there's food in your kitchen cupboard! And if you run out, you can go to the store for more!

Then consider that some human minds—guys like Joseph Nicéphore Niépce and Louis Daguerre—invented the camera so we could preserve visual images on paper to look at again later. How does that happen?

And think about glass! It's solid, but you can see through it! What? How? Wow!

Finally, don't even get me started on the senses—tasting, seeing, feeling, hearing, and smelling. Or the way the earth rotates on an axis of exactly 23.5 degrees to provide us with four seasons.

Friends, I think we need to spend more time being amazed. I think we need not just to notice creation, but to follow King David's example: "I will meditate on your majestic, glorious splendor and your wonderful miracles" (Psalm 145:5 NLT). And make sure that includes the miracle of everyday stuff we take for granted.

Atheism is in vogue these days. We listen politely as scientists explain how the universe came into being. How refraction creates a rainbow. How armadillos survived because evolution gave them armor plates. Evolution also led to our five senses and ligaments in our fingers that allow us to grasp, twist, and twirl a shoelace. The tilt of the earth is a happy accident.

There is a grain of truth woven into most scientific arguments. But is it unreasonable to consider the possibility of a master designer? There is no possible way random and chaotic units of matter could have just fallen neatly into place to create this amazing, beautiful, strategically cohesive universe.

If you believe otherwise, you haven't been paying attention. Creation points to God. As Romans 1:20 explains, "Since the creation of the world God's invisible qualities—his eternal power and divine nature—have been clearly seen, being understood from what has been made, so that people are without excuse."

In summary, those who look around and allow themselves to reflect on the magnificence of creation have no choice but to conclude that God is designer, builder, and master. Anyone who fails to get that idea must be distracted. Either they are bored with nature and take it for granted, or they are so busy trying to prove there is no God that they miss the glory and generous gift he has given to all humankind.

Let's not take anything for granted. Neither the routine nor the astounding. Twentieth-century author and theologian G.K. Chesterton wrote, "We should always endeavor to wonder at the permanent thing, not at the mere exception. We should be startled by the sun, and not by the eclipse. We should wonder less at the earthquake, and wonder more at the earth."

Checking the List

God is present and visible in the smallest one-celled creature and the universe itself. If you look, you'll see.

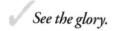 *See the glory.*

Count the Cost

When I was about 12, our family decided we were going to cut back—just a little—on the extravagance at Christmas. In an attempt to refocus on the true reason for the season, we were committed to piling not quite so many presents under the tree. Furthermore, the six of us would all draw names and make a homemade gift for one person. A charming idea, don't you think?

Well, this middle school boy picked Dad, and I ambitiously set out to craft a wooden chess set for the man who had taught me to play. We already had a nice solid wooden chessboard, so all I had to do was cut, carve, and stain...well, 32 chess pieces. To make a long story very short, I didn't quite finish the task. I made one pawn. And that was that. On Christmas morning, Dad unwrapped his gift. I sincerely promised to finish the entire set, but I think he knew it was never going happen. Clearly, I didn't count the cost.

In Luke, we find out that I'm not alone in my failure to anticipate how much work it takes to complete a task. Jesus describes a scenario that at first looks like instructions to architects and building project managers.

> Which of you, desiring to build a tower, does not first
> sit down and count the cost, whether he has enough to

complete it? Otherwise, when he has laid a foundation and is not able to finish, all who see it begin to mock him, saying, "This man began to build and was not able to finish" (Luke 14:28-30 ESV).

Counting the cost is good advice when you're building a tower, crafting a chess set, planning a vacation, applying to colleges, or dreaming about retirement. Like so many other truths presented in the Bible, that's a pretty good lesson for life. But if you read the passage in context, you'll see it's much more than a simple lesson about budgeting your time, talent, and treasure.

Jesus is talking about the cost of following him.

This 2000-year-old speech was delivered to a large crowd that had been traveling with Jesus, and it may have been a direct challenge to those who were tagging along merely out of curiosity. His call was for discipleship—complete devotion and recognition that you can't be a part-time believer. In the surrounding passage, Jesus describes how you may have to turn your back on your family. You have to separate yourself from the world. You should even expect to be persecuted for your faith.

Is that bad news? Not at all. There's zero satisfaction in living a wishy-washy life. Jesus's message is to go big or go home. And go in with your eyes open.

When you start building a life in Christ, you eventually want to come to a full awareness of what's expected, and you want to finish strong. Throughout the Gospels, Jesus confirms that he wants you to find joy, satisfaction, and purpose in life. But it comes with a price: full and complete surrender. He explains, "Whoever finds their life will lose it, and whoever loses their life for my sake will find it" (Matthew 10:39).

That warning—to surrender 100 percent—is for your own good as well as your witness to others. As the above passage from Luke describes, you could spread out blueprints and boast about your big plans, but if you don't complete the job, you are leaving yourself open for some serious ridicule. Anyone who leaves a tower only half built will be mocked.

Now you could respond, "Who cares what other people think?" But you should care. It does matter. The Christian life should be attractive. We need to walk with confidence and purpose. We live with the knowledge that great things are waiting for us. We are going to finish what we start. Seekers and skeptics should look at the lives fully built by Jesus and say, "I want what they have."

Checking the List

Counting the cost to follow Jesus sounds like some kind of business transaction. And it is! He is ready to trade his life for yours. That's right. You are worth Jesus. That's the best deal you will ever find. Because of his sacrifice, he can offer you a one-way, nonrefundable ticket to eternity. As Jesus said—his last words on the cross—"It is finished." He held up his end of the deal. How about you?

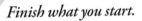 *Finish what you start.*

Quit One Thing

There is a new and worthy obligation coming up on your calendar. But you are absolutely dreading it.

For days, weeks, or years, it will surely suck up a lot of your brainpower. You know the event (or series of events) is worthwhile, and lives may even be changed because of it. But you don't have the time. You don't have the energy. There are just too many other deadlines, activities, distractions, and crises looming large in your life.

You made the commitment in good faith. You even felt that God was calling you to this work. It feels like your sweet spot. You've made an assessment of your talents, experiences, and spiritual gifts. This project uses all of them. You also know that as hard as it is to carve out the time, once you're there, you'll be glad you stuck with it. Still, this exhausting event simply doesn't fit in your current schedule.

You know what you have to do, right?

Listen carefully. Whatever it is that has come to mind, please *don't quit*. Instead, quit *something else* to make room for this larger-than-life project. That's right. There's a reason you have not yet abandoned this project. A significant part of you wants to invest your gifts and talents in this fresh, new mission.

It might be an outreach at your church, a service project in the community, coming alongside a neighbor or relative in need, a far-reaching missional undertaking that brings people together, or an activity only you can do all by yourself but simply must get done. You may be in charge. You may be a quiet, dedicated worker among many. You may get grand kudos just for showing up. You may get no thanks at all because no one in this world even notices.

Your initial instincts are not incorrect. For people who are overcommitted, *saying no to new projects is often the best choice.* But it's not easy. The problem is your many gifts and your generous heart. Plus, your friends, family, community, and world are counting on you. How can you turn them down?

As difficult as it is, an honest assessment will help you realize that when you're spread too thin—trying to do too much—something has to suffer. Something is going to be pushed off to the side. Often that's your family because after all, they *have* to love you. Sometimes it's your job, and that's not quite fair to your employer. Frequently it's your health. Exhaustion and frenzy go against your doctor's orders.

And of course, in the midst of your busyness, you spend less time listening to God just when you need him most.

Ironically, when you say yes to too many things, you're actually saying no to everything. There are only so many hours in a week, so you end up doing nothing well. Which means everything suffers.

The answer is obvious. You just never wanted to make the tough call. To make room for new growth, you need to be ruthless about pruning one or two branches that promise to be less fruitful during this growing season.

What should you quit?

How about that short-term volunteer position that turned out to be a long-term position? You knew it wasn't a good fit four years ago, but you raised your hand because no one else had the guts, and the work had to get done.

Maybe quit the outreach, small group, or club that has taken a nasty turn. The original mission has long been forgotten, and recent meetings are pretty much all gossip, wheel-spinning, self-aggrandizing, or idle talk about weather, business, or politics.

Maybe you can respectfully step down from a leadership position while recommending someone new to take the reins. Identify a qualified successor, offer a giant dose of encouragement, and then get out of the way. Make yourself available as an advisor, but don't be surprised if the organization does just fine with a new leader. And that's a good thing.

Perhaps you're doing something that takes you five hours every week that really isn't necessary anymore. Transportation, purchasing, idea sharing, publishing, so much technology, and your own family situation have changed dramatically in the last decade.

Examples? High school athletic booster clubs used to print out directions to fields at "away games." Google Maps makes that obsolete, saving time and money. Similarly, there's no longer any need to typeset, print, and mail newsletters or membership lists. Of course, instead of driving across the state to pick up those weekly supplies, you can have them delivered to your doorstep the very next day. And if your kid has graduated from Awana or Pioneer Clubs, maybe it's time to step aside. (Or not.)

In most cases, you really shouldn't even think of yourself as *quitting*. You're just replacing something worthwhile with something even more worthwhile.

Checking the List

You are not the same person you were just two years ago. You've learned new stuff and gained new skills. To be honest, so have the other people in your circle. New opportunities arrive. Old expectations depart. Quitting something that has run its course in your life may be the most productive thing you can do today.

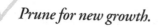 *Prune for new growth.*

Plan Your Escape Route

If you're living by yourself in a first-floor apartment and can simply climb out your window in the event of a fire emergency, then you probably don't have to spend a lot of time planning an escape route. Nevertheless, please make sure you have a working smoke alarm, never dry your underwear in the microwave, and promise me you won't pass out drunk while smoking in bed. But you already know all that.

However, if you live with your family in a multilevel house with younger kids or older adults, you will want to give this warning some serious thought. The National Fire Protection Association offers a 19-point step-by-step strategy for making sure everyone in a burning building has the best chance to get out safe and sound. That includes walking your family through your home and identifying exits, testing smoke alarms, explaining how to check doors for heat before opening them, practicing crawling below smoke in hallways, and arranging for a group meeting place at a lamppost or driveway across the street.

Formulating an escape plan in case of fire should definitely be on your to-do list. But actually, that's not what this short chapter is about.

Your to-do checklist should include planning an escape route that is, perhaps, even more important than any strategy proposed by the NFPA or your local fire chief. It's about escaping the universal problem of temptation.

We all have them. We all face them with varying degrees of failure and success. We all have one or two or three categories of temptations to which we are most likely to succumb. I won't draft a long list of possible temptations here. For one thing, there are too many to name. Plus, if I failed to include your most vexing temptation, you might think you were off the hook. Which of course is not true. On the other hand, naming it would only make you feel guilty. And that is rarely helpful.

What I can confirm is that there is a way out. If you let him, God will show you a path around, over, or quickly through any temptation. The Bible delivers this clear promise:

> No temptation has overtaken you except what is common to mankind. And God is faithful; he will not let you be tempted beyond what you can bear. But when you are tempted, he will also provide a way out so that you can endure it (1 Corinthians 10:13).

That's good news, right? To confirm, you don't have to live in constant fear of being tempted. Yes, you will face temptation. You're human, so that's guaranteed. (Even Jesus was tempted during his forty days in the desert before beginning his public ministry.) But you can claim victory over Satan's whispers. Not by yourself, but with God's help.

Just like preparing for a worst-case-scenario fire in your home, you'll want to do some careful planning. Recognize the areas in your life where you are vulnerable to temptation. Physically remove yourself from situations that foster temptation. Recruit trusted friends to hold you accountable. Turn away *early* from minor temptations—before you plummet down any slippery slope. Meet with other overcomers for strength and encouragement (as long as it doesn't become a gathering of enablers).

Finally, pray the Lord's Prayer often, emphasizing that remarkably prescient request, "Lead us not into temptation, but deliver us from the evil one."

Checking the List

Fleeing temptation is one of those activities many of us know is in our best interest but still fail to achieve with a high level of success. Maybe that's because we wait until we're in the moment of seduction, fascination, or entrapment. Staying in tune with the Holy Spirit will allow us to put down the matches before the fire starts. That will prevent us and those we love from getting burned.

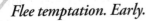 *Flee temptation. Early.*

Speak into the Life of Another

You may recognize the name Dwight L. Moody as the founder of the Moody Bible Institute and Moody Publishers in Chicago or perhaps the greatest evangelist of the nineteenth century. Before film, television, or streaming video, Moody preached the gospel to more than 100 million people in tents, church buildings, town squares, and battlefields across Europe and America.

Many recite his quotations even though they don't know the source. Here are eight thought-provoking quotes from D.L. Moody worth mulling over and hanging on to.

- "The Bible will keep you from sin, or sin will keep you from the Bible."

- "I believe Satan to exist for two reasons: first, the Bible says so; and second, I've done business with him."

- "There's no better book with which to defend the Bible than the Bible itself."

- "There are many of us that are willing to do great things for the Lord, but few of us are willing to do the little things."

- "Where one man reads the Bible, a hundred read you and me."

- "I know the Bible is inspired because it inspires me."

- "We can stand affliction better than we can prosperity, for in prosperity we forget God."

- "Character is what you are in the dark."

An inspiring and challenging quote often attributed to Moody is one he would emphatically confirm was spoken by another man. It was British revivalist Henry Varley who said, "The world has yet to see what God can do with a man fully consecrated to him."

Varley spoke those words in a private conversation to his new friend D.L. Moody during an 1872 revivalist crusade in Dublin. Moody took that one-sentence challenge to heart, and it motivated his ministry for the rest of his life. A year later, Moody would say this to Varley:

> Those were the words sent to my soul, through you, from the Living God. As I crossed the wide Atlantic, the boards of the deck of the vessel were engraved with them, and when I reached Chicago, the very paving stones seemed marked with "Moody, the world has yet to see what God will do with a man fully consecrated to him." Under the power of those words I have come back to England, and I felt that I must not let more time pass until I let you know how God had used your words to my inmost soul.[1]

Varley was touched and honored to be used by God in that way. But—and here's the takeaway for all of us—Varley recalled spending time in conversation with Moody, but *he didn't remember speaking that life-changing quote.*

That's right. Henry Varley could not recall saying the most inspiring and constructive words ever to come out of his mouth. And maybe neither will you. You may never know how your words impact the trajectory of another person's life.

The British preacher was obedient in his ministry. Made friends with people who were also obedient in their ministry. Spoke from his heart. And let God do the rest.

On your to-do list for this week is to do the same. Ask God where you should go, and then show up and speak words of encouragement. Not idle chatter. Not false praise. Not long speeches that demonstrate how smart you are. Shoot for simple truths that apply to the life or circumstance of a friend, family member, colleague…or even a stranger with whom you strike up a conversation. Because you never know.

If you're not good with words, borrow someone else's. You can't go wrong respectfully quoting Scripture. You may already have a favorite inspiring phrase on a poster, plaque, or screensaver that's worth sharing. Maybe use one of the D.L. Moody quotes listed above.

Or like Henry Varley one and a half centuries ago, keep doing God's work and then turn to the person working right alongside you and let God speak through your voice. Without even knowing it, you may change history.

Checking the List

By the way, D.L. Moody was in Dublin because his church had burned down in the Great Chicago Fire of 1871. Which only adds to the idea that we never know how and where God is working. We just need to be faithful.

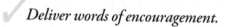 *Deliver words of encouragement.*

Take One Step Back

Despite the title of this book, this chapter gives you permission *not* to do something great today. Really, it's okay.

As a matter of fact, most of your time and effort should be spent not doing great things, but instead doing what needs to be done to lay the groundwork for great things.

In sports, it's called practicing. Developing new skills. Plotting new strategies. Making small adjustments to your technique. Ingraining them to muscle memory through repetition. Breaking down muscles so they regenerate stronger. The adage has validity: Practice makes perfect.

In road construction, taking one step back means motorists will endure a frustrating summer of bright orange warning signs and bumper-to-bumper traffic so they can enjoy a wider, smoother, faster road in the fall. Or maybe the following fall.

In manufacturing, taking a step back might mean expensive retooling. Sacrificing profits this year for a more productive future.

In warfare, it might mean retreating to a fortified position in order to better assess your own strengths and your opponent's vulnerabilities.

Parents of teenagers may find themselves enduring a season in which their son or daughter loudly expresses how they do not appreciate their choice or style of discipline. Later, with any luck, those young

adults will realize Mom or Dad was just protecting them from the fol-
lies of youth and providing them a solid foundation for life. In that
case, the entire family goes through a process of tearing down in order
to grow stronger in the long run.

The idea is to take one step back now in order to create the opportunity to take two steps forward later.

This principle also may have significant application when it comes
to your personal faith journey. There's value in retreating to a quiet
place to study, pray, read Scripture, and listen to God. Asking life's
deepest questions and uncovering unshakable answers. That's really
the only way you can be ready to defend your faith and speak the truth
with confidence.

In many ways, walking into a church sanctuary for worship, hearing the Word, wrestling through theological issues, taking communion,
and fellowshipping with other believers is a step back. Like a football
team in a huddle before lining up for the next play, you're coming
together to lay groundwork. The ball doesn't move during the huddle. Forward motion toward the goal happens only when each player
receives his assignment, trusts the coach, understands how he fits into
the big picture, and executes on behalf of the team.

So here's the big question. Tonight, when your head hits your pillow and you look back on your day, can you honestly say you either did
something great or prepared to do something great? Or did you pretty
much waste a day's worth of oxygen?

There's no guilt here. It's just that you shouldn't take this chapter as
an excuse for a lackadaisical life of backsliding or passivity. True, you
don't have to cross the goal line every day or even get a first down. But
every day you are expected to practice, strategize, assess your strengths
and weaknesses, retool, reinforce a foundation, or huddle with teammates. It's all about laying solid groundwork for the future.

Here's another way to look at it. By taking one step back, you can
remove yourself from any immediate conflict, burden, or expectation.
That allows you to take a breath and view the world from a slightly

clearer perspective. With a fresh focus from a new angle, you may even get a tiny, brief glimpse into God's perspective. And that's great news. Proverbs 5:21 tells us, "A man's ways are before the eyes of the LORD, and he ponders all his paths" (ESV).

Want to do great things? God is continually scoping out all your options, and he promises to send you down exactly the right path. But he may not give you that assignment until you take a step back. Because then you will be fully prepared to move forward in great leaps and bounds.

Checking the List

If you find yourself charging unprepared into enemy territory, I applaud your ambition. But if you get shot down, beaten up, or eaten alive, maybe it's time you took a step back. Feed your soul. Sharpen your sword. Plan your attack. Find a mentor. Partner with a fellow warrior. And then forge ahead.

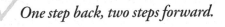 *One step back, two steps forward.*

Escape the Echo Chamber

It sure is nice when people agree with you, isn't it? You feel good about yourself and your ideas. You move ahead with your plans without any hesitation. And the future unfolds without a hitch. Or maybe not.

When we surround ourselves with yes-men—people who agree with everything we say and do—we are pretty much guaranteed to fall short of God's plan for our lives and personal ministries. Why? Partly because two heads are better than one. By surrounding ourselves with people who have different experiences and education, we'll hear a variety of opinions and can choose the best. Also, we should never forget that we live in a fallen world, and our own thought patterns and motivations will never measure up to God's best.

Publisher and blogger Art Rainer, writing on the topic of church leadership, warns about the negative effects of living in an *echo chamber*—an environment in which only your own ideas are heard and considered. He suggests it's a good thing when a leader's decisions and actions are challenged and others are allowed to pitch ideas. Rainer describes four dangers for leaders whose work environment has become an echo chamber.[2]

Good ideas will go unspoken. Echo chambers develop not because of the team's love for their leader but because of their fear of him. A team member may have a better idea but won't share it.

Echo chambers perpetuate a team's lack of trust in their leader. As an echo chamber persists, the likelihood of a team member questioning their leader dwindles. And so does the trust in the leader's ability to do what is best for the organization and for each team member.

Echo chambers inflate the leader's ego, making them a worse leader. Leaders in an echo chamber will quickly convince themselves that their ideas are truly best. They will begin to think they have all the answers. They will be stripped of humility, leading to the absence of listening and empathizing.

Because at some point, the flaws will be seen. It won't be the team members that reveal the leader's flaws—it will come from someplace else. A bad decision will be made, and someone from the outside, where there is no fear of the leader, will speak honestly and without reservation. And the leader will try to determine how he got himself into the situation to begin with.

Leaders aren't the only ones who find themselves living in an echo chamber. Many of us read or listen only to ideas that match our own. Our social circles and social media all echo the same message. We flourish on the affirmation and begin to believe we already have all the answers. Which means we stop pursuing truth or thinking new thoughts.

In many ways, we do have access to ultimate truth and guidance. As Christians, we have the Bible, the Holy Spirit, prayer, and the wise counsel of mentors, pastors, and accountability partners. But our *interpretation* of what we hear from those sources can be corrupted by the limitations of our earthbound reality. Isaiah 55:8-9 explains it well: "'My thoughts are not your thoughts, neither are your ways my ways,' declares the Lord. 'As the heavens are higher than the earth, so are my ways higher than your ways, and my thoughts than your thoughts.'"

In other words, we need to aspire to have the mind of Christ but never assume we have achieved it. Anyone who thinks they are 100 percent heavenly minded is probably no earthly good.

So how do we escape the echo chamber? What might be on God's to-do list when it comes to listening and learning? It might be to accept the fact that our own voice can lead us astray. We need to stop being smug or self-righteous because we all still have much to learn.

It's very possible that we just need to listen more to the wisdom, experience, and opinions of those around us. Outside the echo chamber, we will hear someone who disagrees with our point of view, but that's often a good thing. You don't have to change your mind, but you do need to hear them out.

Or maybe the item on our to-do list is to stop blowing smoke or kissing up to someone in authority. You are doing them no favors. And your own wisdom and experience is being wasted.

Checking the List

Fight to the death for those core truths you know are indisputable. But for most of your ambitions, allow humility and curiosity to open the door to fresh winds and inspirations. You don't have all the answers. You're not home yet.

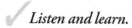 *Listen and learn.*

Thank Your Parents

Imagine calling your mom or dad and just saying something like this:

"Hi. It's…" (Insert name.)

"I've been crazy busy with…" (Give a brief description of one of your current projects. Make it mostly good news with a positive spin because parents hope the best for their kids and want to have happy news to brag about with their friends.)

"For the last few days I was thinking about you and just wanted to call. How are you doing?" (Then listen. If your parents have good news, respond with words like "that's great." And if they deliver some sad news, share their sorrow or concerns and ask a few follow-up questions that confirm you care.)

"I wanted to tell you some news and get some advice…" (Deliver a legitimate piece of news about something meaningful going on in your life. Then ask for their opinion. It could be about a career move, relationship, household project, vacation destination, medical issue, or legal question. The goal is not to worry your parents. It's to make them feel valued…and you might get some solid advice.)

"And hey, I talked to…" (sibling, uncle or aunt, old family friend) "…and it sounds like they're doing well. They said to say hi to you." (Parents like to think their kids keep in touch with family and friends. It's part of the legacy they are leaving.)

"Well, that's all for now. Looking at the calendar…" (If you can end with a promise or intention to see them in the near future, do that. If there are no plans, you can speculate on some future holiday or travel plans. But don't make a promise you have no intention of keeping.)

"It's always good talking. Maybe I don't say it enough, but I love you and appreciate all you've done. I still need you. Thanks for being there. Take care."

Make sense? Is this something you can do? Or should do? This is not about guilt or repentance. This is about family.

Speaking as a father of adult children, I'm sure your parents are rooting for you to do great things. We don't expect you to put your life on hold for us. We don't need to hear every detail of your day. But as I tell my kids, "Throw us a bone every once in a while."

If you live three states away, that's even more important. If we know you're going through a life crisis, let us know what we can do. You're still our kids. If some bad blood or harsh comments from the past are still hanging in the air, I encourage you to do or say what you can to put those feelings behind you. Don't necessarily expect a torrent of emotional apologizing and weeping and hugs. (There could be, but there doesn't have to be.) Families can sometimes leave things unsaid and move forward without dredging up and belaboring regrets from the past. After all, "Love covers over a multitude of sins" (1 Peter 4:8).

Of all the things on your to-do list from God, this one really might be an item to check off this week. And every week for the foreseeable future.

Speaking as a son who lost both my parents in the past few years, I will always be grateful for the intentional time I put in to connect with my folks. Some of it was obligatory because of circumstances, but even that turned out to be a blessing.

Which brings us to the fifth commandment: "Honor your father and your mother, so that you may live long in the land the Lord your God is giving you" (Exodus 20:12). Or as I like to misinterpret the passage, "Be nice to your folks and get real estate."

Checking the List

Call your parents. Or stop by. If it's not easy to call for "no reason," you can wait for Mother's Day or Father's Day. But *today* might be just the right day.

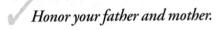 *Honor your father and mother.*

16

Do What You Can

God's to-do list for your near future will contain only stuff you can do, not stuff you can't do. Because you *can't* do stuff you can't do and you *can* do stuff you can do. Make sense?

Let's break that down into six very short blurbs: Accept the assignment. Clarify the calling. Take responsibility. Keep learning. Ask God to expand your responsibilities. Be a team player. And we'll even add a little biblical support to each of those six points.

Accept the assignment. When God gives you a project, don't go sniffing around to see if someone else has a more fun or more important job. You've got your assignment. Do it. And do it well.

> "Whatever you do, work at it with all your heart, as working for the Lord, not for human masters, since you know that you will receive an inheritance from the Lord as a reward. It is the Lord Christ you are serving" (Colossians 3:23-24).

Clarify the calling. God doesn't want you spinning your wheels. So set high expectations and forge ahead. Suddenly finding yourself in a sweet spot—doing good work that matters—is the best way to confirm your calling.

"Be all the more diligent to make certain about His calling
and choosing you; for as long as you practice these things,
you will never stumble" (2 Peter 1:10 NASB).

Take responsibility. Be a faithful steward of the many gifts and talents
you've been given. Please don't sell yourself short or whine about having too many responsibilities. God knows your exact capacity. You've
got more to give, so you've got more to do.

"When someone has been given much, much will be
required in return; and when someone has been entrusted
with much, even more will be required" (Luke 12:48 NLT).

Keep learning. Start by doing what you can. Then listen to those with
experience. Learn from your mistakes. And suddenly you will increase
what you can do.

"Whoever heeds instruction is on the path to life, but he
who rejects reproof leads others astray" (Proverbs 10:17 ESV).

Ask God to expand your responsibilities. God is not going to give you
more than you can do. He will stretch you. He will challenge you. But
along the way, he will also equip you with resources and partners who
will come alongside to help with your expanding responsibilities. Don't
be afraid to pray like Jabez:

"Jabez cried out to the God of Israel, 'Oh, that you would
bless me and enlarge my territory!'" (1 Chronicles 4:10).

Be a team player. You may have a healthy self-image...or not. Either
way, you are just one player in this game with a whole bunch of folks
doing their best with a variety of gifts. Some gifts may seem more
important than others, but they aren't!

"Do not think of yourself more highly than you ought, but
rather think of yourself with sober judgment, in accordance

with the faith God has distributed to each of you. For just as each of us has one body with many members, and these members do not all have the same function, so in Christ we, though many, form one body, and each member belongs to all the others. We have different gifts, according to the grace given to each of us" (Romans 12:3-6).

Here's the deal. Don't worry so much about what you can't do. Or what you don't know. Don't let anyone put you in a box. Don't think you have all the answers.

Just do what you can.

Checking the List

You are being recruited. There are tasks to be done and souls to be saved. "[Jesus] said to his disciples, 'The harvest is plentiful but the workers are few'" (Matthew 9:37).

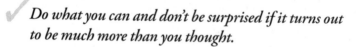 *Do what you can and don't be surprised if it turns out to be much more than you thought.*

First, Do No Harm

About four centuries before Jesus, Hippocrates, the father of medicine, founded a medical school on the Mediterranean island of Kos. As you might imagine, physiology and medical science have come a long way since then. Hippocrates advanced the idea that a person's health required four bodily fluids—blood, phlegm, yellow bile, and black bile—to be kept in balance. As a result, bloodletting and purging were common practices. Which meant patients seeking help from the well-intentioned doctor didn't always make it home alive.

Despite his long-disproven medical theories, a version of the Hippocratic Oath still exists today. Oaths like this one are not legally binding and are mostly symbolic, but many medical schools have graduating students recite oaths that provide valuable guidance as graduates move into the practice of medicine. These token declarations reference the need for respecting life and protecting patient confidentiality, and they emphasize that *preventing* disease is actually preferable to *curing* disease.

Famously, one of the tenets of the Hippocratic Oath is "First, do no harm." Today's medical professionals debate the authorship of those four words—and their accuracy. After all, surgeries begin with making an incision, beneficial drugs often have negative side effects, and experimental treatments sometimes do cause harm. One interpretation of "First, do no harm" is to acknowledge that in some cases, the best plan of action is no medical intervention at all. Instead, doctors simply provide comfort and control pain.

I believe the concept of "first, do no harm" has a valuable application to authentic Christians. Which, by the way, is why I don't have a fish on my car.

Allow me to explain. It's entirely possible that identifying yourself as a Christian may not be recommended. Especially if you're a jerk.

You may recall that chapter 6 challenged you to shine—to exhibit enviable character traits, model love and generosity, and give glory to God for how he is working in your life. When you shine, you draw others to God.

Conversely, when someone who calls himself a Christian changes lanes too fast, blows through a yellow light, tailgates, and makes rude gestures to other drivers, his actions can have the opposite effect. Obnoxious behavior or dangerous driving by someone pulling out of a church parking lot with a WWJD bumper sticker gives atheists ammunition and seekers one more reason to doubt.

So that's one of the best reasons I can think of to clean up your act. It's all about your witness. You don't want to give Jesus or his followers a bad reputation. Certainly, being a Christian isn't about putting on a show of piety or pretending that your life is perfect and problem-free. But we should make it a definite goal to *do no harm*.

So what's a follower of Christ supposed to do if they dishonor, diminish, or disgrace themselves? What if you or I fail by displaying anger, gossiping, falling to an addiction, betraying a confidence, lusting, lying, or worse? Thankfully, there is a way to turn that negative into a positive. And you already know what you have to do.

You have to make things right. Acknowledge your misdeeds. Clean up your mess. Sincerely ask forgiveness. Make restitution. Take steps to prevent yourself from backsliding. Surprise any offended or damaged party by turning your back on that sin.

When the time comes, don't make that apology about you. Ground yourself in humility and find grace. Then give the glory to God.

Keep "Do no harm" on your to-do list. But add this: "Model repentance."

Checking the List

Keep doing your best. But when you fail (and you will), be broken by that sin, atone, and make amends. Your humble repentance may be the greatest evidence of Christianity some people will ever see.

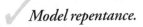 *Model repentance.*

Choose a Life Verse

Want to start an interesting dialogue with another believer? Ask, "Do you have a life verse?"

For a book project several years ago, I asked that very question of a slew of fascinating people, triggering some great responses and a few surprises.

What's a life verse? Well, it's a short excerpt from Scripture that has a special meaning to that individual. It might be a verse God provided at exactly the right time to help them through a tragedy or challenge. It may have helped them cast or crystallize a vision for their personal ministry. It could be a verse given to them by a grandmother or favorite teacher. Often, it relates directly to a turning point in their lives—perhaps their moment of salvation. Paradoxically, a life verse may change over the course of a life. Early on it might be about you. Later, you might choose a verse relating to others. A few examples might help.

Joni Eareckson Tada relates that after a reckless diving accident left her a quadriplegic, she would wake up in the morning and cry out, "Oh God, I can't live this way…I don't have the strength to face a life of paralysis." That's when she found her life verse. Second Corinthians 12:9 (NLT) says, "My grace is all you need. My power works best in weakness."

Joni writes, "It began to dawn on me that my weakness might very well turn out to be a strength—it would force me into the arms of Jesus

out of sheer desperation. And I learned that's not a bad place to be."
Joni's ministry continues to touch millions.

Charles Colson, former chief counsel to President Richard Nixon
and founder of Prison Fellowship, recalled a moment in his third day
at Maxwell Federal Prison Camp. Moved to read his Bible, he found
Hebrews 2:10-11:

> In bringing many sons and daughters to glory, it was fitting
> that God, for whom and through whom everything exists,
> should make the author of their salvation perfect through
> what he suffered. Both the one who makes people holy and
> those who are made holy are of the same family. So Jesus is
> not ashamed to call them brothers and sisters.

Colson suddenly realized the murderers and drug dealers with
whom he shared incarceration were brothers, sinners like himself, and
still loved by God. In that moment, Colson's life found new purpose.

James MacDonald had accepted Christ as a boy but vividly recalls,
"I was returning to the Lord at seventeen years of age after an extended
period of rebellion. My heart was aching and famished because of the
way I had starved myself spiritually." He couldn't get enough of God's
Word—just like the prophet Jeremiah, who wrote, "When I discov-
ered your words, I devoured them. They are my joy and my heart's
delight" (15:16 NLT). Today, a commissioned representation of that
verse by calligraphic artist Timothy Botts greets Pastor McDonald as
he enters his study.

As an atheist, legal scholar, and news journalist, Lee Strobel spent
nearly two years investigating the evidence for Jesus. Alone in his bedroom on November 8, 1981, he found himself drawn to John 1:12: "To
all who did receive him, to those who believed in his name, he gave the
right to become children of God." Lee suddenly noticed that the key
words of John 1:12 formed an equation of how to become a follower
of Jesus: Believe + Receive = Become. His story is documented in his
book *A Case for Christ*.

Do you have a life verse? Reading these examples, perhaps a person-ally significant portion of Scripture has risen into your consciousness. Go ahead and claim it as your life verse. Meditate on it. Consider how it fits in the context of Scripture and the context of your life.

Don't panic if you can't identify the perfect verse. And feel free to change your life verse as your life evolves. A life verse is not like a tat-too that's difficult to remove. But I do encourage you not to take this assignment lightly.

When you settle on your own life verse, commit it to memory. Read it in multiple translations—NIV, NLT, ESV, NASB, KJV, and so on—and choose the one that works well for you. Also, read it in context and see what a few Bible commentators have to say about that verse so you fully understand the meaning at its deepest level. Then go ahead and share it with a few people in the next week or so.

And if we cross paths, I hope you'll share your life verse with me. I'll share mine with you!

Checking the List

Of course, all of God's Word has application to our lives. But there's something satisfying and enriching about uncovering one small portion of the Bible and claiming it as your very own. Maybe even encourage others in your circle of influence to identify their own life verse.

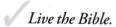 *Live the Bible.*

19

Pray as Modeled

That to-do list God has for you today most certainly includes prayer. And you can't go wrong using the mnemonic device ACTS: Adoration. Confession. Thanksgiving. Supplication.

The word "adoration" reminds us that God is worthy of praise and his awesomeness should bring us to our knees. He's not just more magnificent than the Grand Canyon or Niagara Falls, he is the *Creator* of those natural wonders. If we start our prayers with humble adoration to a glorious God, we're headed in the right direction.

Confession breaks the hold of sin in our lives so we can pray from a clean slate. God already knows where we fall short of his glory, but doing our own personal inventory will surely lead to an attitude of repentance. Confessing our sins begins the process of breaking the pattern of sin. The exciting news is that when we come to God for forgiveness, he has already forgotten our sins, casting them away "as far as the east is from the west" (Psalm 103:12).

After we acknowledge God's grandeur and come clean before him, it's natural to give thanks. Thanksgiving for life. Thanksgiving for supplying all our needs. Thanksgiving for the good stuff and the bad, because he uses it all to make us more like him.

Then there's the idea of supplication—praying for God to keep doing what he's already doing. It's actually a little silly to think we have any idea of what we should be requesting as we pray. God knows exactly what we need. His plan is perfect. If it were up to us, we would be asking for stuff we *think* we need, but we would probably be wrong. So let's make sure we include prayers of trust along with prayers of request.

You may have never considered this before, but ACTS is actually modeled by Jesus himself when he offered us the ideal prayer in Matthew 6:9-13:

> In this manner, therefore, pray: Our Father in heaven, hallowed be Your name. Your kingdom come. Your will be done on earth as it is in heaven. Give us this day our daily bread. And forgive us our debts, as we forgive our debtors. And do not lead us into temptation, but deliver us from the evil one. For Yours is the kingdom and the power and the glory forever. Amen (NKJV).

Three of the letters in praying ACTS are easy to identify. Adoration: "Hallowed be Your name." Confession: "Forgive us our debts." Supplication: "Your will be done…Give us this day our daily bread…Deliver us from the evil one."

It may seem odd that the Lord's Prayer does not explicitly include any thanksgiving to God. But maybe the entire prayer is overflowing with a spirit of gratitude. We're thankful that God is engaging us from heaven. We're thankful he provides our every need and forgives our trespasses. We're thankful for his guidance and protection. Even the Hebrew word translated "amen" means "so be it" or "truly." Saying "amen" confirms our acceptance, respect, affirmation, and appreciation for what was just spoken.

Modern theologian R.C. Sproul, founder of Ligonier Ministries, endorses ACTS and offers this reminder:

> I think this is a helpful acrostic for remembering both the elements and the priorities of prayer. Unfortunately, we often spell our prayer life something like SCAT, because

we start with supplication and spend very little time, if any, on adoration, confession, and thanksgiving.[3]

There are scores of excellent resources on praying more deeply, wisely, humbly, and so on. Prayer really is a form of surrender to God's will for our lives. And that needs to be foundational and foremost on our to-do list. Today and every day.

Checking the List

Prayer changes things. James 5:16 says, "The effective, fervent prayer of a righteous man avails much" (NKJV). That idea should be a source of great comfort—but maybe not to everyone. Like so much of Scripture, you have to actually read and consider the words. Prayer will avail much, but only prayers from those men and women who are *righteous* and willing to pray *fervently*.

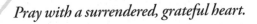 *Pray with a surrendered, grateful heart.*

Pray This Very Moment

Have you done this too? During a conversation, a friend or acquaintance shares some challenge they're facing. A situation at work. A sick kid. A rough patch in a marriage. A family member going through a crisis. A wayward teen. A personal spiritual desert. Something that could use some serious intervention from the Creator of the universe. Because I believe in the power of prayer, I would say, "I'll pray for you."

Then I would break that promise.

It wasn't intentional. It wasn't a lie. So why didn't I pray? Maybe I got distracted by a personal emergency. Maybe that promise to pray got sidetracked by an even bigger prayer request. Maybe I was being a little selfish because I have a tendency to think more about myself than about others as I move through the day. But really I meant to pray, I wanted to pray, and sometimes I did remember to pray. But not as often I wanted. As I said, way too frequently I would fail to keep my promise.

You may be nodding your head because you've done the same thing, so let's consider a few strategies we could use to fix this obvious shortcoming. How about pulling out a notebook from a pocket, purse, or briefcase and jotting down the name, date, and prayer request? Then make it a point to go through that list once a day or several times a week.

Another option would be to pull out your smartphone right then and there and use one of the prayer apps that help you track your prayers and remind you to pray. Apps like PrayerMate, Echo, Pray with Me, Prayer Notebook, or Prayer Journal. Some of those apps include a verse or short teaching of the day, updates from missional organizations, the ability to track answered prayer, and the ability to forward prayer requests through Twitter, Facebook, and so on.

One possible strategy would be to spend intentional time at the end of every day recalling all your personal interactions. That would include waving at your neighbor, tickling your toddler, talking to Mom on the phone, texting your BFF, yelling at that referee, cursing the driver in the giant SUV, walking quickly past the panhandler, kissing your spouse, giving an ultimatum to your teenager, reading about the president in a news magazine, talking with your old work colleague, and tipping that barista who was obviously having a bad day. Some or all of those individuals need your prayer.

In one sense, all you have to do is say, "Heavenly Father, everyone I met today—please draw each one them close to you. Amen." He knows their exact needs, and he will honor your prayers. But there's something satisfying about submitting our specific, thoughtful requests to an all-powerful, all-knowing God. He wants us to dig deep into our own heart and be fully aware of the needs of others. Prayers need to be grounded in devotion, humility, and sincerity.

Making scribbled or digital notes requires you to take immediate action by pulling out your phone or journal. Making a nightly "needs review" requires you to think about every twist and turn of your day, and you'll inevitably miss someone or some need.

Every sincere prayer strategy is valid, but the best plan of action might be to pray right then and there. Why wait? You can certainly still put any need on your prayer list. And you can still review your day as you slip into bed. But praying in the moment invites God's intervention that much sooner.

As you pass that friendly neighbor, pray for him. As you kiss your spouse, pray for your marriage. As you curse the gal who cut you off in traffic, pray for her...and yourself. Pray for that grumpy barista as you take your first sip of coffee. Pray for your children during every interaction. When your old work chum talks about the mess he's made of his life, ask right then and there, "Can I pray for you?" He will say, "Umm...sure." And then take it to God. In that moment, you'll know what to say, and your friend will have joined with you in that prayer as well.

Checking the List

Of course, you don't have to pause to pray. Prayer should be an ongoing component of every moment of the day. The idea is confirmed in that seemingly impossible command in 1 Thessalonians 5:17, "Pray without ceasing" (NASB). But really, it is quite doable because we're in constant connection with God through the indwelling of the Holy Spirit. Make sense?

 *Pray right then and there.*

Live with Sin

Our goal is to live without sin. But that is impossible.
As long as we live in this fallen world, we are surrounded and influenced by sin. And yes, we will continue to sin.

In Romans, Paul famously writes, "What I am doing, I do not understand; for I am not practicing what I would like to do, but I am doing the very thing I hate" (Romans 7:15 NASB).

That seems like terrible news, and Paul's tone seems agonizingly distraught, but this kind of realization is actually good news. Paul's statement confirms he is *recognizing* the sin in his life. That would be a huge victory for any of us! He also seems to be saying he is *grateful* for the law because it points out how far he has fallen. In Romans 3:20 he explains, "Through the law we become conscious of our sin."

So that's one more reason to dig into Scripture and listen to preachers who aren't afraid to talk about God's law. Sin drags us down. It distracts us from our purpose. It steals our joy. By knowing the law, we have a fair chance of avoiding some of those sinful patterns. When we identify our hidden weaknesses and our most difficult temptations, we have a chance to steer clear of them. As an experienced farmer might say, "To keep from stepping in the manure, you have to know where it is."

That strategy actually works for everybody. Anyone who was so inspired could make a long list of biblical laws—including the Ten

Commandments—and that would be a pretty handy blueprint for staying out of all kinds of trouble. Lying, stealing, coveting, lusting, and so on bring disharmony to human relationships. A more satisfying life awaits those who avoid sin.

But there's even better news. Authentic Christians have an additional warning system—the Holy Spirit. Galatians 5:16 gives this helpful recommendation: "Let the Holy Spirit guide your lives. Then you won't be doing what your sinful nature craves" (NLT).

Coming full circle in this chapter. Please don't put "live a sin-free life" on your to-do list. It's not possible. You're only setting yourself up for failure. Only one person ever made that happen. Thankfully, he's on your side and lovingly shares his victory over sin and death with you.

Moving forward, here's the plan. Accept Jesus's offer to pay the price for your sin with his blood. That settles your debt and opens your life to the Holy Spirit. Then, empowered by the triple-threat blessing of the Trinity, go to battle against sin. It's not a losing cause. You may have to live with sin, but you can also see progress as the sin in your life begins to diminish. Really.

As described above, I think you can claim victory every time you *recognize* sin. As you live the examined life, you can also claim victory when you find yourself sinning *less frequently*. In addition, you frustrate Satan any time you sin *less severely*.

Does that make you shudder? Does the idea of sinning less feel unworthy of applause? How can any sin—even a rare and small one—be considered a victory? Asking those questions is another indicator that you're moving closer to God. That's always a good thing.

An example might help. Pick your sin of choice. Anger. Gluttony. Gossip. Pride. Whatever. Let's say you find yourself in a situation in which your normal response always has been to sin and sin big. But then something kicks in and you back away. Maybe it's a still, small voice, a wave of fear or regret, a verse you've memorized, a promise recalled, a revulsion of the person you have become, or some other message from God. That's good news, right?

In this world, sin happens. That's no excuse for plopping down into a cesspool of filth and surrendering to the darkness. Think of it this way: The fact that we face sin every day gives us a daily chance to choose the better path. That's something we can live with.

Checking the List

We're not home yet. Living without sin and the temptation of sin is one more reason to look forward to heaven. But for now, let's pledge to recognize sin, sin less frequently, and sin less severely. Deal?

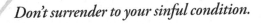 *Don't surrender to your sinful condition.*

Don't Get Sideswiped

You're on a multilane expressway going about four miles per hour faster than the posted speed limit. There are cars on all sides, but that's okay because you're all traveling en masse. The drivers are all staying out of each other's blind spots and moving at the same rate of speed. Except one joker. He (and it's usually a guy, but not always) is doing a high-speed, highly dangerous bob and weave. He's tailgating, accelerating, braking, and changing lanes as if his life depended on it. Funny thing—lives actually are hanging in the balance as he performs his stunt driver maneuvers. Except he's not a professional driver, and he's not on a closed track.

How should you respond? Give him room. Plenty of it. Don't beat him. Don't join him. He's destined for a literal heap of trouble, and you want to be far, far away when he finds it.

Here's the item for your to-do list. Keep that same response in mind for most of the overzealous, overanxious, overaggressive hooligans who race through your life thinking of no one but themselves. Simply get out of their way.

In a classroom, they're the ones who profess to know more than the teacher, dominate class discussions, and never acknowledge the opinions of others. On a sales team, they're the ones who squawk until they get the best sales territory and wouldn't stop for three seconds to help a rookie salesperson. On a sports squad, they get more playing time than they deserve simply because the coach mistakes a loud mouth for enthusiasm.

It might not seem fair, but often these weasels do get to their destination faster, sell more product, and lead the team in one or two stats. But leaders they are not. As a matter of fact, these selfish miscreants can take away from the team, drag down a company, and steal the joy from any group experience.

How you respond makes all the difference. First, expect to run into these characters once in a while. Second, remember the lesson from the expressway. *Give them room.* Don't let them sideswipe you, and don't get caught in their fiery pileup. Third, make friends with your other teammates by staying positive and resisting the rottenness of the one bad apple. Fourth, do your job to the best of your ability, finding satisfaction in having your priorities in order.

Finally, search your own heart. Are you one of those selfish tailgating hooligans? If so, congratulations for surviving this far. But know that your luck won't last.

Checking the List

When you see short-term success for anyone who isn't playing fair, you may be tempted to mimic their methodology. Please don't. The Bible warns, "Where jealousy and selfish ambition exist, there is disorder and every evil thing. But the wisdom from above is first pure, then peaceable, gentle, reasonable, full of mercy and good fruits, unwavering, without hypocrisy" (James 3:16-17 NASB).

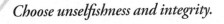 *Choose unselfishness and integrity.*

Speak the Gospel

For several years, on the sink in our guest bathroom, we had a cute little framed quote attributed to Francis of Assisi that read, "Preach the gospel at all times; if necessary, use words."

A few things about that little bit of bathroom decor. One, I'm not sure where it came from.

Two, it's not there anymore. My bride, Rita, moves things around when I'm not paying attention, which is one of the many things I love about her. (Unless it's footstools or end tables being moved, which I tend to trip on in the dark of night.)

Three, as a guy who likes words, I am delighted with the wordplay. The comparatively short sentence includes a challenging imperative with personal application; not one, but two dramatic pauses; surprising verbal irony; and a rare semicolon, used properly.

Four, historians doubt that Francis of Assisi said it. There's no record of it in his writings. And despite his meek reputation, Francis was a fiery orator and knew the value of words.

Five, it's not true. Certainly, you can reflect the gospel in the way you live your life. Your actions can lay the groundwork for someone else to be receptive to the gospel. But to actually deliver the gospel *requires words*.

For the record, here's one way of using words to deliver that message:

God created you and loves you. But our sin—our rebellion—separates us from God, and the penalty for our sin must be paid. God loves us so much that he sent his Son to pay that price by dying on the cross. It's a gift. It's grace. It's not something we can buy or earn through good works. Jesus rose from the dead, proving he is the Son of God and has power over sin and death. If we believe in Jesus, desire to turn from our sins, and accept his gift, he will forgive our sins, provide us with a new sense of purpose in this world, and welcome us into heaven someday.

That's the gospel. The good news. Yes, there's a lot there. But for someone to truly accept Christ as their Savior, they have to pretty much understand all of this. They may not grasp it all at once. Any presentation of the above concepts may open the door to questions and doubts that all must be addressed. Which may require even more words.

There are those who say the 26 words in John 3:16 are all you need to pierce hearts and bring people into the kingdom. That's certainly a valid point. I also am not going to argue with the legendary British preacher Charles Spurgeon, who was asked to put the gospel in as few words as possible. He replied, "I will put it in four words for you: Christ died for me."

In most cases, I am a proponent of fewer words. *Less is more* is one of my life principles. But when it comes to delivering the gospel, let's make sure we have the right words—the complete story—ready when the time comes.

Going back to that quote falsely attributed to Francis of Assisi. Mime, telepathy, or wishful thinking is a bad plan for delivering the greatest news the world has ever heard. Absolutely, we need our actions to be bold, inspiring, loving, and compelling. We should be so alarmingly generous, kind, and compassionate that everyone we meet is stunned by our generosity, kindness, and compassion, and they are moved to implore, "Tell me, please! Why in the world are you so generous, kind, and compassionate?"

That's when the best kind of evangelism occurs. *Hope-filled actions followed by welcoming words.* The ideal circumstance is described well in 1 Peter 3:15: "Always be prepared to give an answer to everyone who asks you to give the reason for the hope that you have. But do this with gentleness and respect."

Checking the List

Our lives should "preach the gospel at all times," and our voices should be eager to instruct, clarify, invite, and welcome another soul into the kingdom of God.

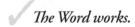 *The Word works.*

Stop Saying "God Is Good" When Good Things Happen

Are you one of those well-intentioned, generally optimistic Christians who says, "God is good" every time something pleasant or lucky happens?

A parking spot opens right in front of the bagel shop. The sun breaks through the clouds just as you take your seat at Wrigley Field. The nasty neighbor with the yapping dog puts up a "for sale" sign in front of his house.

During these wonderful, satisfying moments, if you say, "God is good," you are absolutely correct. Because God *is* good.

But I hope you agree, if you circle the block seventeen times and finally give up on grabbing a tasty treat at your favorite bagel shop, God is still good. If you take a day off work and sit through four rain delays, only to watch the Cubs lose, God is still good. And if your neighbor doesn't move, but instead buys three pit bulls that howl all day and spread terror on the sidewalks, God is still good.

That's right. God is good all the time. All the time, God is good.

Saying those three words after a joy-filled or satisfying experience is easy and obvious. May I suggest that there's no reason to say it? As a matter of fact, making that statement after a delightful experience could imply that when things are not going your way, God might not be so good after all. And that's dangerous ground.

Let's consider the opposite scenario. Sometime tomorrow you suffer a minor personal setback. You lose a client to an unethical competitor. Your cupcakes burn. Your car gets towed. In that moment, if you can whisper to yourself, "God is good," then you might be well on your way to rescuing the day. The world is not ending. You will survive.

Then take it even one step further. The truly courageous and forward-thinking follower of Christ might ponder, *I wonder how God is going to use this disappointment or frustration to bring glory to himself?* You may discover that God can use you to model true faith and advance his kingdom.

After losing that client, you gather your colleagues and announce the bad news while confirming your commitment to integrity and fair play. Your four-year-old sees that you *do not* curse your burned cupcakes. That's a win right there. When you go pick up your car from the auto pound, you treat the agent with dignity and respect. That probably doesn't happen too often.

Remember. All good things and only good things come from God. That's true even if our meager human minds don't understand it.

This conversation wouldn't be complete unless we opened our Bibles to Romans 8:28: "In all things God works for the good of those who love him, who have been called according to his purpose."

If I read that right, God uses good things for good. He uses mild discomfort for good. And he uses tragedy for good. That sounds like an unbelievable promise and incredibly good news. However, taking a closer look at that second part of that verse, there seem to be some strings attached. Bible scholars suggest that the promise to work out everything fine and dandy is made *only* to those individuals who truly love God and also are being drawn to God through the Holy Spirit.

That includes my family and me. And hopefully, you and all those you care about. In the moment, we may not see how God is working, but we can trust that he is.

In summary, it really is a wonderful and accurate truth to say, "God is good." Anytime. But how about if we double the number of times we say it? In good times and bad.

Checking the List

When it comes to the existence of an all-powerful God, people often stumble over the question, how can a loving God allow bad things to happen to good people? The simple answer is, we're not home yet. For now we live in a fallen world, and bad things sometimes happen to all people. Plus, bad things allow Christians to demonstrate to the world how to respond to setbacks when your ultimate hope is in God.

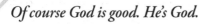 *Of course God is good. He's God.*

Clear the Clutter

By now you can tell that many of the chapters in this book take a popular make-your-life-better strategy found in self-help books, blogs, and magazines…and turn it upside down.

So it is with this chapter. "Clearing clutter" is trending big right now. Spend a few minutes online or in the checkout line at the supermarket, and you will read a wide assortment of headlines about tidying up your life, getting organized, or busting the clutter. Well, that is certainly a great idea. If your sock drawer, closet, or kitchen cabinets need a good purging, then go for it.

Of course, the Bible never says cleanliness is next to godliness. But it surely makes sense to keep a tidy home and spend reasonable effort caring for your possessions. After all, who really needs fifty pairs of shoes or two drawers of socks? Hoarding broken appliances, stacking old newspapers to the ceiling, renting storage lockers for stuff you will never use again…these habits are dangerous, wasteful, and a little worrisome. So go ahead and eradicate some of the physical debris from your life.

But don't stop there. Or maybe don't start there. Much more important than your physical space is your spiritual, emotional, and mental space. One of the very first items on God's to-do list for your life should be clearing the clutter out of your heart, mind, and soul.

There's plenty of biblical support for this idea.

- "Don't be so concerned about perishable things like food. Spend your energy seeking the eternal life that the Son of Man can give you" (John 6:27 NLT).

- "Be careful, or your hearts will be weighed down with carousing, drunkenness and the anxieties of life, and that day will close on you suddenly like a trap" (Luke 21:34).

- "Sell your possessions, and give to the needy. Provide yourselves with moneybags that do not grow old, with a treasure in the heavens that does not fail, where no thief approaches and no moth destroys. For where your treasure is, there will your heart be also" (Luke 12:33-34 ESV).

As citizens of earth, it's way too easy to focus on things that don't last or activities that lead to partying, boozing, and stressing. That kind of clutter doesn't just eat up your time, money, and productivity. It also distracts you from heaven. As these verses suggest, it's a trap and a losing proposition.

What earthly activities should we be expurgating? The list is long, but not really surprising: Old habits we know are bad news. Old regrets we dwell on. Old temptations we should be avoiding. Old judgmental attitudes that hinder us from making new friends. Old fears we could turn aside simply by seeing the bigger picture. And even old relationships that influence us to make decisions we shouldn't make.

A few moments of self-examination will help you fill in personal specifics. Names, places, websites, addictions, attitudes, and temptations quickly will come to mind. How long have these habits and burdens been holding you back?

It's time to clear that clutter. When things that don't last are finally out of the way, your vision will no longer be blocked. You will more clearly see your heavenly home. God's plan for your life will come into focus.

Do not conform to the pattern of this world, but be transformed by the renewing of your mind. Then you will be able to test and approve what God's will is—his good, pleasing and perfect will (Romans 12:2).

If this short chapter leads you to fill a dumpster in your driveway, that's a solid win. But if it leads you to turn your heart, mind, and soul away from this world and toward heaven, that's a grand victory for the kingdom of God.

Checking the List

Most of us have way too much stuff. And there probably is a connection between our worldly possessions and our relationship with God. So maybe today—or in the next few months—commit to purging a bunch of the unnecessary stuff from both your physical and spiritual life.

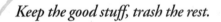 *Keep the good stuff, trash the rest.*

26

Do Stuff No One Does Anymore

It's entirely possible that I am being way too nostalgic here. I pride myself on being realistic and certainly won't deny the value of progress and technology. But there are things the next generation might never experience that were valued activities to past generations. Plus, change isn't always better. Some traditions should be cherished. Technology occasionally seems to bypass some of our senses. And staring at screens is not the same as experiencing the real world.

Do any of these make sense to you? Or maybe you're ready to dump every one of these antiquated customs without fanfare and move into a more productive yet soulless future.

Write in cursive. I fear that the next generation of children won't be able to read or write cursive. Is that important? Losing that skill would essentially mean great-great-grandma's prairie diary and John Hancock's signature at the bottom of the Declaration of Independence are illegible scribbles.

Talk on the phone. I would much rather talk on the phone than text. Emojis will never replace vocal expressiveness. Texts will always be misinterpreted, and brief digital blurbs can never really embody a heart-to-heart conversation.

Mail Christmas cards. Doesn't it warm your heart to go to your mailbox in December and get something besides junk mail and bills?

Play Scrabble. As wedding gifts, Rita and I may have given away thirty or more Scrabble games along with a modest check tucked inside the card. We're just trying to encourage couples to spend time together with less noise and a dash of fun competition.

Write a letter. When's the last time you wrote a letter? On paper? And mailed it?

Bring a plate of cookies to the new neighbor. This great tradition gives you an excuse to find out more about the family that just moved in.

Read a newspaper delivered to your doorstep. More in-depth than TV news. More eclectic than the stuff that shows up on Internet news feeds. Plus you get local politics, comics, puzzles, and an excuse to sit at the kitchen table and drink a second cup of coffee.

Drink regular coffee. Percolate a pot at home for 20 cents per cup. Cheaper. Fewer calories. And on occasion, when you do spend $4 on a cup of fancy coffee, it will once again feel like a splurge.

Sit under a tree and journal. Imagine how fun it would be to read what your father wrote in his youth. Or how fun it would be in twenty years to read about what you did this summer! Journals or diaries are treasured forever.

Use cash. When you slide or insert a plastic card into a kiosk, you're less aware of how much you're spending. Handing over five or six twenty-dollar bills from your wallet to pay for dinner out is a reminder of what dining out really costs. (Or maybe you don't want to think about it.)

Hang laundry outside on a clothesline. You're not going to do this. It's just not practical. But pillowcases and bloomers blowing in the breeze create an iconic image from the last century worth remembering. Can't you just picture a soldier coming home from World War II surprising his young bride as she hangs the laundry in their side yard?

Offer to pray. Sometime in the last decade or so, members of the media stopped saying, "Our thoughts and prayers are with you." After hearing of some tragedy or difficulty, an interviewer or even a newscaster would say those gentle words as a way of expressing a caring attitude and inviting the greater community to follow up with prayer. Apparently, two of those seven words ticked off some atheists. And I guess that's understandable. So now we only hear, "Our thoughts are with you." I think it's probably okay if you and I go ahead and pray anyway. Even without that nudge from the media.

Watch a movie as a family. In most families, everyone has their own screen(s) so they can watch what they want when they want it. Movies on TV used to be events that brought families together. Even bringing home a movie from Blockbuster was a big deal. No more.

Check a map. It's now common to fly into a city, rent a car, follow routing instructions from a disembodied voice, and never really know where you are. Unfolding a map gives your destination a sense of dimension, direction, and relationship to the rest of the region and state.

Ride bikes to a friend's house. Do kids ride bikes anymore? Some families do bike trails. But I rarely see nine-year-olds on bikes. And I live in a city that *Family Circle* magazine recently named the best city in America to raise a family.

Use recipe cards. Cookbooks are wonderful tools. And I encourage you to find creative new recipes online. But handwriting an old family recipe on a three-by-five card to pass on to someone who admired your dish or dessert is an honor and responsibility.

Book your vacation through a travel agent. You can book most trips online yourself. But a travel agent may know a unique getaway and a moneysaving deal you could never find on your own. Just call and give a local agent your travel dates and your budget and say, "What do you recommend?"

Send a postcard. A cheap souvenir that says, "We're here and you're not!"

Memorize six phone numbers. Your sweetie. Your parents. Your BFF. Your boss. Your favorite pizza joint. And your own. Someday you may have to use someone else's phone or be allowed only one phone call from prison.

Save up for something you really want. Most of us buy things on credit way too haphazardly. If you really want a sailboat, motorcycle, leather couch, subzero fridge, Alaskan cruise, or ski trip to the Swiss Alps, try saving your nickels for a year or so. That strategy also cuts back on impulse spending.

Gather photos in an album. Would you rather swipe through a phone full of self-indulgent selfies and poorly framed images or turn through page after page of memories and cherished moments? Don't trust the cloud. Like so many items in this list, there's security and comfort having a book, map, pen, journal, or photo album in your hand.

Go to a bookstore. One of the great joys of life is browsing the aisles and seeing what's new. And maybe even buying a real book to take home or give to a friend.

I sincerely hope a few of the above activities make it on to your to-do list. As you mull over this list, if any other endangered activities come to mind—especially ones you cherish—track me down and share them at jaypayleitner.com.

Checking the List

There's no reason to fear the future. Or curse technology. But let's not change for the sake of change. Or abandon things that bring people together and spread a little joy.

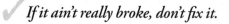 *If it ain't really broke, don't fix it.*

Buy a Used Tuxedo

High school talent shows reveal a wide range of "talents." Audience members may be genuinely moved to tears by the beauty of a haunting cello solo or the grace of a young ballerina. A powerful dramatic soliloquy by a shy sophomore may surprise the entire student body. A future comedian will get his share of laughs, but most of the jokes will likely fall flat. In quite a few schools, the event will include a magician, an athletic jump rope artist, and a fairly entertaining rap inspired by *Green Eggs and Ham* or *Goodnight Moon*.

You can expect some too-loud screeching from a rock band assembled just for this talent show. With only one rehearsal, a few members of the football team might successfully perform a crowd-pleasing song and dance. You can also count on several acts that consist mostly of lip-synching, although I'm not sure that's a real talent.

The most memorable high school talent show I've attended included most of the above. But the favorite act of the crowd packed into the high school gymnasium that evening was my son Max displaying his extraordinary ability to catch marshmallows in his mouth when they're thrown from a great distance.

The idea and execution was all Max. His athleticism and confidence had been honed over years of excelling in organized baseball, wrestling, and football. His ability to catch popcorn, sunflower seeds, ice cubes, and M&Ms in his mouth had been sharpened in dugouts and locker rooms and at my own kitchen table.

The plan was coming together nicely. After the emcee's introduction, he would walk into the spotlight carrying a guitar case, open it, and pull out a 20-ounce bag of Kraft Jet-Puffed Marshmallows. He had already recruited his older brother, Randy, to come home from college to be the official marshmallow thrower. On cue, circus music would play while Randy tossed marshmallows to his little brother. They would begin just six feet apart, but after each throw, Max and Randy would each step back and widen the gap until Randy was throwing those white confections the full length of the basketball court.

One minor question was left unanswered. A couple of Max's friends were sitting in our kitchen making suggestions about what Max should wear during his performance. A football jersey? A sport coat? A clown costume?

When teenagers sit around a kitchen table, a parent might be in the same room but not really be part of the conversation. I interrupted the brainstorming by saying something like, "How about a tuxedo?" That idea was well received, but everyone agreed the cost of renting a tux was probably not worth the impact. I replied, "Give me a day or two. I have an idea."

So I called the local tuxedo rental franchise, talked to the manager, explained the situation, and reminded him of all the tuxedos that store typically rents to high school boys during prom season. I said I didn't need to rent a fancy new model for $150. I just wondered if they might *sell* an older model that was just sitting in the warehouse for half that amount.

Well, the tuxedo store manager came through, and Max looked dashing. His marshmallow catching act earned a standing ovation. Of course, it would have regardless of what Max was wearing. But the tuxedo added a nice bit of flair and drama to the evening.

To be clear, I had nothing to do with the original idea, the tossing, or the catching. I just happened to be there when Max was brainstorming with his friends. And Max was open to my minor involvement. As a result, the final outcome was enhanced.

So how does "Buy a Used Tuxedo" fit onto your to-do list? Well, there are two parts to this story. (1) Be willing to share an idea, and (2) be willing to consider it.

With some projects, you may be inclined to go it alone, block out distractions, and finish the task without any assistance. That might be the best way to take ownership and complete your vision. But in most cases, it's wise to keep the door open for suggestions and addendums from friends, colleagues...and even dads.

For example, I'm not sure who suggested the idea of an assembly line to Henry Ford or the TV remote to Zenith. But breakthrough concepts that improve on your original idea can come from any source. If you're willing to listen.

Just as important as receiving tweaks and suggestions is having the courage to make them. How often do you have an idea on how to make someone else's project a little bit better, but you hesitate to make the suggestion? No one wants to be laughed at. Or ridiculed. Or ignored. And there's always the fear that your idea might actually be implemented...and fail.

But that's the joy of being part of a team where you can give and take ideas. You feel comfortable putting in your two cents to make someone else's core idea ever so much better. It's not about who gets credit. It's about surrounding yourself with people you trust *and* who trust you. That's how great ideas come to life.

When you buy a used tuxedo, the risk is small and the reward is sweet. If it works, you get to play a small role in a memorable endeavor. Everyone wins.

By the way, once a young man has a tuxedo in his closet, it's amazing at how often it gets used. But that's another story.

Checking the List

Surround yourself with friends and colleagues who can give and take ideas freely without fear of judgment. Take advice. Give credit. Explore options. Be silly. Encourage creativity.

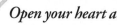 *Open your heart and mind to new ideas.*

Pick Up the Slack

My dad had a fish pond just behind the house. It wasn't one of those fancy-schmancy, multilevel architectural marvels laid out by a waterscape design firm. This little pond was my dad's own design and execution. An oval pool about six feet across lined with a sturdy tarp and just deep enough that it didn't freeze over the winter. It had a single pump that recirculated water down a modest waterfall cascading along a stack of limestone rocks. Whenever a grandchild or two came over, they'd head out back to Papa's pond and feed Papa's goldfish, even if the fish had already been fed that day. Each autumn, Dad would scoop out all the smaller goldfish but leave a couple of the bigger ones who were strong enough to survive a Chicago winter. Sweeping the snow off the ice, it was always amazing to see the fish—not frozen solid, but floating motionless in a state of suspended animation.

Year after year, the pond was a joy-filled hobby for my dad. Which is why it was so disappointing for him when his cancer and other illness left him unable to do the necessary maintenance. I lived in the same town but was too busy, too shortsighted, and too selfish to even realize what was going on. The little pond needed lots of TLC—pump maintenance, algae prevention, leakage control, occasional fish carcass removal, and much more.

My brother quietly stepped up. Without any fanfare, whining, or glory hogging, Mark pulled up on that gravel driveway several times a week, walked around back, and surveyed Papa's pond. Sometimes he was there ten minutes. Sometimes he invested an entire Saturday doing what needed to be done. For three, maybe four years, Mark made sure that the view out my parent's back picture window was not a decaying, overgrown disarray of crumbling rocks, hoses, tarp, and fading memories. Instead—when Papa felt up to the challenge—it was a place he could still visit while steadying himself on the arm of one of his growing grandkids. As if they were trained, those goldfish would burble up to the surface, hoping to snack on floating food pellets. Papa and his grandkids could still feed the fish. And they did. Even if Mark had already fed them earlier that day.

I never even saw the need. (Or maybe I pretended I didn't see the need.) Thankfully, Mark saw and followed through. Season after season. That kind of vision accompanied by action is definitely on God's to-do list for each of us.

So where might you pick up the slack? That expression might seem to suggest that someone has dropped the ball. That whoever was in charge of a necessary job stopped doing it because of laziness or allowing some distraction to get in the way. But really, "picking up slack" is just the nature of the seasons of life. For instance:

Vance is taking classes toward his MBA on Tuesday nights, so someone else needs to pick up the slack and take the garbage cans to the curb.

Sharon gets a full-time job, so someone else needs to call bingo at the nursing home on Monday afternoons.

Cameron volunteers to help at the Bible camp on weekends, so someone else needs to step up as head usher at church for the summer.

The World War II veteran who organized the Memorial Day tribute at the local cemetery for the past four decades passes away, so someone else needs to step up, or that tradition will surely fade away.

What other real-life examples come to mind? Is there something in your home, neighborhood, or community that used to get done—but for some reason is no longer getting done? If you see it, do you ignore it? Or do you say, "Here I am, Lord, send me"?

This week—on your personalized to-do list—there may not be any critical needs to "pick up the slack" that require your attention. But stay aware. Opportunities come without warning. If you hang out with good-hearted people who seem to be always thinking of others, you will discover plenty of chances to suddenly serve.

Last thought. There's extra satisfaction if you do those deeds without any fanfare. A trait exhibited by my brother Mark and his selfless pond maintenance. Matthew 6:1 recommends, "Take heed that you do not do your charitable deeds before men, to be seen by them. Otherwise you have no reward from your Father in heaven" (NKJV).

Checking the List

Is there a regular task that was handled efficiently in the recent past but has been neglected for a while? Such as changing furnace filters, dandelion control, driveway sealcoating, or fence painting? It could be in your own home or some other location. Maybe the task requires some human interaction, such as visiting a shut-in or volunteering at a shelter or crisis center. Where can you pick up the slack?

 *Be part of the solution.*

Get Past Your Past

Will all perfect people please raise your hand? Anyone? I didn't think so. Okay, then. Now we can start this short chapter. Acknowledging that you've made mistakes is a great place to start anything. It reminds you that you can't get through this life on your own.

Even better than admitting mistakes is truly confessing those sins and asking for forgiveness. That's your best strategy for leaving the crud behind and moving into a fresh-scrubbed future. Let's take a life-giving look at a few passages from Scripture that will help anyone get past their past.

> "If anyone is in Christ, the new creation has come: The old has gone, the new is here!" (2 Corinthians 5:17).

This may be the most hope-filled verse in the Bible. You can be made new. Clearly, the first step in putting your past behind you is to accept grace. With Christ as your Savior, you can truly start fresh.

> "Forget the former things; do not dwell on the past. See, I am doing a new thing! Now it springs up; do you not perceive it? I am making a way in the wilderness and streams in the wasteland" (Isaiah 43:18-19).

After chastising the nations of Judah and Israel for 39 chapters, the prophet Isaiah instructs them to wipe their rebellious ways from their memory. Even when we are in the desert, God promises us guidance and provision for our deepest needs.

> Brothers and sisters, I do not consider myself yet to have taken hold of it. But one thing I do: Forgetting what is behind and straining toward what is ahead, I press on toward the goal to win the prize for which God has called me heavenward in Christ Jesus (Philippians 3:13-14).

This New Testament verse reminds us that while we have a long way to go, we have what it takes to press on. Once again, the theme is forgetting what is behind and looking ahead. Heaven awaits.

One biblical character who refused to be defined by her past was Rahab. When we first meet her in the second chapter of Joshua, she is immediately described and defined by her occupation: Rahab the prostitute. The Bible doesn't sugarcoat it. There's no confusion about what she did, her reputation, or her place in society.

But when two spies sent by Joshua to Jericho were looking for a place to hide, God led them to her apartment, which was built into the walls of the city. Rahab—a pagan, Canaanite, and prostitute—had heard about the power God had already displayed in the region. She was ready for a change. The two men were more interested in her trust than her customary services. The trust was mutual, and it opened the door to Rahab's transformation, a transformation of letting go of her past and looking to the future, which included assuring the safety of her entire family.

Her courage led to her becoming one of the great heroes of the faith. Still, Hebrews 11:31 and James 2:25 refer to her as "Rahab the prostitute." Even after her transformation, why would she carry the label of her past life into the New Testament? Probably to remind all of us that even though we can't erase the past, our personal history does not define our future.

Do you have "fresh start" on your to-do list, but your old self is holding you back? You may not realize it, but many people in the Bible, plenty of the members of your church family, and some folks in your community have overcome painful past lives to become heroes of the faith. This just might be your chance to join them.

By the way, Rahab didn't just change careers. She joined forces with the Israelites permanently. The very first chapter of the New Testament lists her in the genealogy of David, Solomon, and Jesus.

Checking the List

When the walls of Jericho came tumbling down, Rahab left her home and never looked back, truly leaving her past behind. I pray that kind of courage for you.

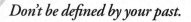 *Don't be defined by your past.*

Try Monotasking

I cannot do more than one thing at a time. Ever. For years, I accepted that as a flaw—a point of shame and embarrassment. But maybe that inability is not such a bad thing after all.

My wife, Rita, is a master at multitasking. I have seen her simultaneously knit, cook dinner, watch TV, let the dog out, pray for a son's job interview, do laundry, respond to urgent city business as an alderman, tell me about her day, balance the checkbook, and somehow also help me with the one thing I'm trying to do at that moment. And she does it all well.

I think Rita may be the exception to this new recommendation for your to-do list: Let's stop trying to do everything at once and start doing one thing well. In other words, let's monotask.

That would mean *ignoring* your phone during a conversation with a friend. *Not* wearing your headphones during your next walk in the woods. Grilling your sweet chili lime chicken with love and care while *someone else* pours drinks and prepares the side dishes. Tucking your kids in bed and *really engaging them* as they share the hopes and fears they experienced during their day.

Doing that one thing—and doing it well—means your friend feels cared for. You actually connect with nature through the sound of the birds, the breeze, and the crunch of leaves underfoot. Your grilled chicken is sweet and moist, not undercooked or burned to a crisp. You have successfully entered into your child's world, and you better understand who they are and what their future holds.

In a remarkably short TED talk—under three minutes—designer and teacher Paolo Cardini promotes the value of monotasking. He admits that it sounds "pretty weird to speak about mono when the number of possibilities is so huge." And he's right. According to Statista, there are well over two million apps available in the Apple App store.[4] Despite that—or maybe because of that huge number of digital distractions—Cardini challenges his audience, "Find your monotask spot within the multitasking world."

The benefits of monotasking are obvious. Better focus. Your workload is better organized. Tools need to be gathered only once. And in some cases—such as driving and texting—multitasking is downright dangerous.

Monotasking may even be a better use of time. Beginning and ending a small project in a single-focused session means you never have to think, *Where did I leave off?* Or *Why did I do that last step?* Once you're at the top of your learning curve, you stay up there until the job is complete. That's much more efficient than stopping and restarting.

Of course, there's value in multitasking. Interruptions happen, and we need to be flexible enough to immediately take care of responsibilities that can't wait. Whether that's a boss who needs a quick consult or a toddler headed for a hot stove. Moms, dads, administrative assistants, teachers, cops, event planners, traffic controllers, waiters, and many other people often have to be master multitaskers.

But mastering the lost art of setting aside or tuning out distractions is certainly worthy of our to-do list. Martial arts action hero Bruce Lee said, "The successful warrior is the average man with laser-like focus." From a spiritual perspective, the ability to focus with laser-like intensity comes in handy when we pray, worship, mentor, disciple, read Scripture, and minister to those in need.

Checking the List

What can you do today to eliminate or minimize distractions and sideshows from your life? Try focusing on one thing with complete concentration and single-minded intensity. Even if it's just grilling chicken, walking in the woods, talking to a friend, or tucking in a third grader.

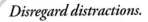 *Disregard distractions.*

31

Take a Fresh Look at Your Favorite Bible Verses

Here's a surprising little exercise for longtime Christians who have a few favorite portions of Scripture committed to memory. Revisit those verses, and you may discover that you have overlooked or forgotten a word or phrase. Some examples may help.

You may be quite familiar with Romans 8:28. "We know that in all things God works for the good of those who love him, who have been called according to his purpose."

The verse is often cited as God's promise that everything we experience ultimately works out for the best. Even terrible tragedies. A closer look reveals this promise to be true, but *only for those who love God and have been called by him.* In other words, authentic Christians can count on this truth. But we probably shouldn't be quoting it to comfort those who do not know God. It doesn't apply to them.

How about Psalm 37:4? "Take delight in the Lord, and he will give you the desires of your heart."

The psalmist seems to be saying that God promises to shower you with your deepest desires. Which apparently could include a new romantic partner, a 1963 red Corvette, a mansion in Beverly Hills, or a couple weeks in Cancun. Are those the "desires of your heart"? Do you think God would make that promise? Actually, Psalm 37:4 is fairly easy to decipher. It hinges on identifying what delights you. If you delight *in the Lord*, then spending time with him and getting to know him reflects your deepest desire—which is to delight in the Lord. See how that works? The more you get to know God, the more you desire to get to know God.

Here's another—Philippians 4:6-7. "Do not be anxious about anything, but in every situation, by prayer and petition, with thanksgiving, present your requests to God. And the peace of God, which transcends all understanding, will guard your hearts and your minds in Christ Jesus."

The frequently overlooked phrase in these verses are the two words, "with thanksgiving." When faced with an anxiety-filled challenge, we can pray to God, and he will bring us unbelievable peace. That's true. But we need to trust God to such an extent that we are grateful for everything that happens to us. Even the unpleasant stuff. We need to bring thanks to God *before* he steps in and cleans up any mess we've made. That's not easy, but that's our assignment.

Finally, here's one more. Hebrews 12:1: "Let us run with perseverance the race marked out for us."

You may think this verse is about endurance. And you wouldn't be wrong. One of my kids had this verse on a poster featuring a lean-muscled runner pounding down a desert highway wearing an expression of absolute conviction.

But did you ever consider the second half of this verse? It suggests there exists a predetermined racecourse. Who marks it out? And is it just for us? The deeper meaning of Hebrews 12:1 might be that perseverance is important—endurance, follow-through, and striving to reach the goal. But it's even more important to identify the right goal God chose for each one of us. You certainly don't want to run with perseverance toward the wrong goal.

What verses decorate your walls, calendars, and key chains? What Scripture have you committed to memory? Open your Bible. Read it fresh. Read it in context. Keep reading it until God reveals a new and unexpected truth.

Checking the List

The word of God is alive and active (Hebrews 4:12). A verse that may have touched your heart years ago could reveal something new and fresh today. For you or someone who needs to hear it. Keep digging. Keep sharing. Keep expecting great things from God.

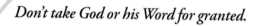 *Don't take God or his Word for granted.*

Wait Twenty-Four Hours

One item on your to-do list for *today* might be to wait until *tomorrow*.

Quite a few things in life can be decided and acted upon in the immediate present. Things like where to go for lunch. Which tie to wear. Whether to stop at the dry cleaners before or after you go to the bank. Whether to delete or open that spam email. Getting a trim. Tossing that expired cottage cheese. What to have on your pizza. Which font to use on the flyer for your lost dog.

Quite a few things should *not* be done on the spur of the moment. Things like getting a puppy. Accepting a job offer. Dropping out of school. Sending that inflammatory email. Asking for a raise. Drastically changing your hairstyle. Shaving your beard. Buying any item over $500. Signing a lease. Signing a multiyear internet and cell phone contract. Going to upper management to report an incompetent coworker. Investing in real estate. Getting a tattoo.

What might you do with that extra day?

Weigh alternate options. Many decisions are made because you think you have only one choice. But that's rarely true. And sometimes the best option is to do nothing. "Wait for the LORD; be strong and take heart and wait for the LORD" (Psalm 27:14).

Consider all possible repercussions. The reason to move forward may be obvious. Your decision will lead to wonderful privileges and rewards. But please consider the downside as well. Puppies are great fun. But they need to be fed, trained, loved, cleaned up after, and occasionally kenneled. For the next twelve years…or more. "Whatever a man sows, this he will also reap" (Galatians 6:7 NASB).

Consider how your choice impacts others. If you do something that makes you feel good, does that mean someone else feels bad? Maybe your significant other really likes your beard or your long hair. Or a work colleague suffers after you quit. Your parents would be broken-hearted if you moved their grandkids to the other side of the planet. For this season of life, the travel requirements for that promotion would be a hardship for your family. Your life overlaps with a lot of people. "Do not merely look out for your own personal interests, but also for the interests of others" (Philippians 2:4 NASB).

Pray. God knows your every need, and he can work in an instant. But he also wants you to search your heart and bring him your burdens and desires. He wants to guide you. Sometimes that takes time. "If any of you lacks wisdom, you should ask God, who gives generously to all without finding fault, and it will be given to you" (James 1:5).

Seek wise counsel. You're a smart person. But on just about every topic, there are people with more experience and valuable insight. Seek them out. "Plans fail for lack of counsel, but with many advisers they succeed" (Proverbs 15:22).

Plan the next step. Only God knows the future. Still, you'll want to anticipate what might happen *after* you make a decision. It's one thing to buy a boat, RV, motorcycle, hot tub, vacation timeshare, or summer cottage. But what other expenses or responsibilities will follow? "The plans of the diligent lead to profit as surely as haste leads to poverty" (Proverbs 21:5).

You don't make major life decisions every day. But they come around more often than you realize. God offers wisdom and guidance from every direction, including the thousands of precepts waiting for you in the Bible. If you don't intentionally and proactively make wise decisions based on God's Word and God's will, unwelcome repercussions will surely follow.

Checking the List

Don't drag your feet. Don't delay decisions out of fear. But give yourself time to make the best determination based on wise stewardship of your gifts and resources and doing work that glorifies God.

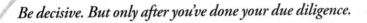 *Be decisive. But only after you've done your due diligence.*

Do Stuff Without Thinking

You've heard the expression, "It's just like riding a bike." In the traditional sense, that phrase means once you learn something, you pretty much know how to do it for the rest of your life.

Well, let's take a few paragraphs to kick around that idea. First, the basic premise is not always true. More than once, I have mastered a piece of software for a project, but a year later I've totally forgotten how to make it hum. For me, working in Excel is not like riding a bike.

Beyond that, the expression probably does have some validity. If you learn something—especially as a youngster—and practice that skill for any length of time, your brain will store that sensory and muscle memory for later use. It might take riding a few blocks on a bike or a few minutes clacking on a keyboard, but you will certainly be up to speed a lot faster than during your original learning curve. There will be some wobbles as you regain confidence and balance. There may be some pauses and missed keystrokes. But most activities learned early and repeated often will come back to you sooner rather than later.

Let's consider a few life skills you could revisit without too much effort after having been away from them for years. Driving a stick shift. Playing scales on a piano. Hitting a golf ball. Ping-Pong. Fielding a grounder. Jacks. Dancing. Skiing. A foreign language you took back in high school.

Imagine walking through your childhood home. Your muscle memory would kick in, and you would instantly recall the cadence of walking up the front steps and the location of every light switch. Your past experiences—especially those you repeated over and over—are part of who you are.

Recently my wife, Rita, surprised herself when she hesitantly went to French braid her hair. She had put her hair up thousands of times when our kids were younger, but she couldn't begin to remember how the swooping, twisting, and tucking actually worked. As she reached back, some mysterious force kicked in, and she had that French braid completed in seconds.

Neuroscientists call this "automaticity" and suggest that it's not literally the muscles that are learning. Rather, the memory is encoded as synaptic connections are strengthened in the brain. In any case, we're talking about repeating a learned motor skill so that it's essentially never forgotten.

So how can this mysterious ability be used for a higher purpose? Well, how about if we list a few repeatable physical activities that could and should become second nature to us? In other words, delightful habits we want to get into.

Such as? Hugging. Blowing kisses. Waving to neighbors. Reaching out to hold hands. Looking up from our screens and smiling when someone enters our space. Putting on our seat belt. Checking our side mirror before opening a car door into the bike lane. Opening doors for others. Offering our seat on a bus. Making eye contact with the person speaking to us. Putting the cap back on the toothpaste. Putting the toilet seat down. (Guys!) Rinsing out cereal bowls and putting them in the sink...or dishwasher. Sharing a hymnal. Waving to a motorist who stopped so you could cross the street. Leaving the TV remote where it's accessible to the next viewer. Pushing your chair in when you leave the table. Turning off lights when we leave a room.

I'm not sure what the neuroscientists would say. Maybe these activities don't all trigger automaticity or memory encoding. Some may be learned behavior, being aware of others' needs, or simply good manners. But I think the idea of identifying uplifting and life-affirming activities and turning them into habits is a worth a try, don't you?

On your to-do list, let's include one or two new habits worth pursuing and begin practicing them. This very day.

Checking the List

This idea of doing stuff without thinking is actually the opposite of acting thoughtlessly. We need to be intentional about meeting other people's needs and even anticipating how we can reflect the love of Christ to those around us—friends, coworkers, loved ones, strangers. The goal is to make our proactive actions second nature.

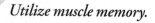 *Utilize muscle memory.*

Grieve that Regret

Already on your to-do list may be a single word: "grieve." I won't ask, but you are well aware of a regret or moment from the past that needs that specific action.

Please understand that God gives you permission to grieve. He wants your broken heart to feel that release. The idea goes beyond mourning the death of a loved one or some other circumstance during which tears are culturally acceptable. Many of us need to weep over something we've kept under wraps for way too long.

As you consider the scope of your life, there may be a real sense of regret at a lost opportunity. Or a season of brokenness that still grips your heart. Or the loss of a relationship from long ago that you never fully accepted. God feels your pain, and he wants to bring you comfort. In most cases, that doesn't mean going around the grief; it means going *through* the grief.

As you read this, what loss has come to mind? Is there a personal failure, deprivation, broken relationship, or squandering of resources in your past? Extreme examples may seem like a movie script, but they do happen in real life. A teenager storms out of the house, and that night a parent dies of a heart attack. A trusted corporate executive gets fired for falsifying a company expense report. A young adult loses an entire decade to drugs or alcohol. A marriage crumbles because of a single foolish act of adultery.

Lives are shattered. Trust and respect are swept aside, instantly replaced with fear, anger, and regret. Recovery seems impossible. Joy seems unreachable.

Some examples of regret underscore the fragility and brevity of life. Imagine a young man being disowned by his father because he chooses not to join the family business. They never speak again, and twenty years later he skips his father's funeral.

Imagine a parent giving an ultimatum: "If you get yourself pregnant, you are not welcome in this house again." What happens when that seventeen-year-old girl faces the anguish of an unplanned pregnancy? Is she homeless? Fending for herself and her unborn child?

Imagine adult siblings never speaking again because their parents' estate plan failed to designate exactly how some of the family heirlooms or investments should be divided. That happens all the time, even if no one really wants the teacup collection or rocking chair.

Other examples may not seem as dramatic, but they touch every family. An education or career path is set aside forever to care for an ailing parent. An invitation lost in the mail leads to unresolved hurt feelings. Best friends go their separate ways because only one makes the team, only one gets into a certain college, or only one gets married.

What have you lost? What do you regret? Maybe you have no desire to open those old wounds. Or maybe you should. John Piper describes a healthy grieving process for the life you had hoped would be.

> I have in mind two kinds of losses: those who had something precious and lost it, and those who hoped for something precious and never had it. It works both ways. Sixty years go by, and forty years on you think, "I've come to terms with that," and then one morning it breaks over you, and you weep about a 40-year old loss, or a 40-year "never have," and my counsel is, yes, go ahead, embrace that moment...

Let there be weeping in those seasons—feel the losses. Then wash your face, trust God, and embrace the life he's given you.[5]

God wants you to weep and then lift your eyes to heaven, rest in him, and soon enough be moving forward again. Invite God along for the walk, and you might even experience a rebirth at the next sunrise. The psalms paint a picture of hope: "Weeping may last through the night, but joy comes with the morning" (Psalm 30:5 NLT).

Checking the List

It's worth remembering that the shortest verse in the Bible tells us, "Jesus wept" (John 11:35). Abraham, Jacob, Joseph, David, Job, Peter, Paul, and scores of others wept. Tears of regret. Tears of sorrow. Tears of recovery. All these people were ultimately used by God and became heroes of the faith.

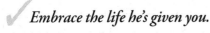 *Embrace the life he's given you.*

Review Your Calendar, Checkbook, and Browser History

You may have heard the decades-old saying, "If you want to know what's important to a person, just look at their checkbook and calendar."

To apply that adage in the twenty-first century, you may want to appraise your browser history as well. Then decide if a thorough review of any of these should go on your to-do list. It's up to you.

First, let's all agree that your time, money, and attention are three of your most valuable assets. Let's also assume that you are typically judicious with your resources. You are intentional about making time to attend third-grade band concerts and arrive early for job interviews. You are intentional about not missing car payments and giving a certain percentage of your income to worthy charities. You are intentional about choosing to read, watch, and listen to things in the digital world only if they instruct and uplift.

Let's also admit that we sometimes drop the ball. Quite a bit of our time, money, and attention is wasted or misused. When we are haphazard with our schedule, investments, and online activity, it's easy to fall into habits that lead down thorny paths, into dark tunnels, and over thousand-foot cliffs.

What kind of things are we talking about? Every person is different. One person's vice may be a beneficial attribute to someone else. Many habits have moral implications. Many of the choices are whims or guilty pleasures. The following incomplete and rambling list includes choices that hijack our time, risk our financial well-being, and take our imagination places we don't want to go. Some items on this list do all three.

Channel surfing. Reading bad romance novels. Spending more than a few minutes every day on social media. Making Starbucks runs. Buying another pair of shoes. Other fashion accessories. Tech gadgets. Collections and hobbies that no longer bring joy. Unending text and email threads. Debating online with lunkheads. Letting meetings go way too long. Thinking every cough is pneumonia and every headache is a brain tumor. Video games. Gambling. The lottery. Reruns. Reality TV. Movie sequels. Movie remakes. Pornography. Catalog shopping. Online shopping. Credit card debt. Celebrity tabloids. Designer clothes. $150 haircuts. $30 cheeseburgers. Bottled water. Power drinks. Convenience store snacks. Junk food. Alcohol. Drugs. Feeling sorry for ourselves. And allowing technology to rule our lives.

This list could have gone on for an entire page, and I may have overlooked your own biggest time, money, and attention waster. And again, not all of these are necessarily vices. I also apologize because some of these concepts probably hit way too close to home. We all know people who have damaged their health or well-being because of some obsession, addiction, or compulsion. Consider this list a diagnostic device to help you consider your own next step.

Which reminds me—whatever your guilty pleasure, it's not my job to tell you to give it up. That's between you and the Creator of the universe. If you think God put "Review your calendar, checkbook, and browser history" on your to-do list, your only responsibility is to *do the review*. By following through, you may discover that your online shopping is actually a timesaver or your latte runs don't need to be eliminated, just cut by 50 percent.

The goal of this review—and most chapters in this book—is to protect your thoughts, time, and treasure. Thereby protecting your heart. As Matthew 6:21 tells us, "Where your treasure is, there your heart will be also."

On the way out the door, you check for your wallet, watch, and phone. Take that as a reminder to check how you use them.

Checking the List

Give your schedule, your investments, and your conscious thoughts to God. He will use them in ways you could never imagine.

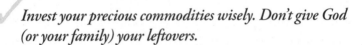 *Invest your precious commodities wisely. Don't give God (or your family) your leftovers.*

Be Ready

Stephen Hawking, the famed theoretical physicist, recently predicted humankind has a mere century left on this earth, more or less. He states, "With climate change, overdue asteroid strikes, epidemics and population growth, our own planet is increasingly precarious."[6]

Well, that sounds good to me. I'm ready. Of course, Dr. Hawking recommends that the human race—or a small contingent of worthy humans—gather our belongings and skedaddle to another planet. If that's your jam, then go for it. Recruiting the optimal men and women for that expedition to save humanity sounds like quite an adventure and a great premise for a sci-fi movie. (I think it's been done.)

But authentic Christians wouldn't have any need to hitch that ride. We understand that Jesus Christ is coming back at the end of the world, establishing a new kingdom on earth, and eventually taking all believers with him to be "caught up in the clouds to meet the Lord in the air" (1 Thessalonians 4:17 NLT).

If I were a biblical scholar or eschatologist, I would now go into a long description of Armageddon and the Day of the Lord. I might enter the debate on whether to expect a pretrib or posttrib rapture. We could also identify possible individuals who might be the antichrist. Adolf Hitler, Mikhail Gorbachev, and Bill Gates have all been ridiculously identified as likely candidates. Every recent American president has been an obvious suspect. Of course, the megaselling Left Behind book series from Tim LaHaye and Jerry Jenkins gave us the fictional Nicolae Carpathia, a lasting archetype for who and what the antichrist might be.

Speculation about the end times is a popular pastime among some folks who are smarter than me. I am clearly not qualified to draw conclusions on such important topics. Besides, *maybe we're not supposed to.* Maybe we're supposed to be working on those things we *can* control. Like our own kindness and truthfulness and love. Sure, debating other believers on specific details regarding the end times can be a nice hobby. But our time might be better spent nurturing compassion for the lost and engaging them in thoughtful discussions about sin, grace, and salvation. (Or maybe doing some of the other 51 things suggested in this book.)

Here's the point. There's all kind of prophecy in the Bible suggesting events leading up to the return of the Savior. Still, no one knows when Jesus will return. "About that day or hour no one knows, not even the angels in heaven, nor the Son, but only the Father" (Matthew 24:36). Other passages remind us that Jesus will come "like a thief in the night" (1 Thessalonians 5:2) and that "it is not for you to know the times or dates" (Acts 1:7). We are to keep watch, but nowhere does the Bible encourage us to discern the time or place of the second coming.

Why the mystery? Clearly, because we shouldn't be waiting around idly. There's work to be done. There are daily opportunities for service and outreach. Not you or me, but some folks might be tempted to keep sinning until right before the deadline and *then* repent. That doesn't sound like a healthy plan.

I understand when people pray, "Jesus, come soon." That day will mark the end of our earthly encumbrances. We are also encouraged and expected to read and understand all of Scripture, which includes the book of Revelation and other biblical passages that point to the end times.

But let's not miss the main point of those passages—the goal of being ready.

Checking the List

The hobby of predicting the rapture is not unhealthy or forbidden in Scripture. But if any debate causes division or becomes a burden to those who seek truth, then maybe we should take a step back and look at the commands Jesus said were the greatest.

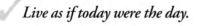 *Live as if today were the day.*

Test Yourself

Y ou may have previously heard this clever quotation. It's a bit flippant, but it makes a valuable point. "Going to church doesn't make you a Christian any more than standing in a garage makes you a car."

And what is that point? Well, there are very likely people in your community who get up on most Sundays and go to church, know a few Bible verses, take communion, put a few bucks in the basket, and volunteer for church events once in a while, but they really aren't followers of Christ.

Just to be clear. Where anyone stands as a follower of Jesus is not my judgment to make. Or yours. As a matter of fact, the only person who can know whether an individual has acknowledged his or her sins, believed in Jesus, and accepted his free gift of grace is that individual himself or herself.

The guy in the next pew who is cheating on his wife? It's not our job to look into his heart and state with certainty whether he is a born-again believer. The woman who visits nursing homes, prays so sincerely in her small group, and gives generously to missionary work? It's not our job to identify her as an authentic Christian. We just don't know. But God knows. And we can trust in him.

Hopefully those individuals know. They know whether they are bound for heaven. But that's not always the case. It's possible that some regular church attendees are fooling themselves, and that can be a little scary. That's why Scripture says to *test yourself.* "Examine yourselves, to see whether you are in the faith. Test yourselves. Or do you not realize this about yourselves, that Jesus Christ is in you?—unless indeed you fail to meet the test!" (2 Corinthians 13:5 ESV).

In the *Redeemer City to City* blog, respected pastor and author Tim Keller references a talk he gave on this very topic not too long ago. Keller offered a series of diagnostic questions he says are "designed to wake up sleeping Christians and to convert nominal Christians." The clear goal is to probe for evidence of how God is working in you and through you.

> How real has God been to your heart this week? How clear and vivid is your assurance and certainty of God's forgiveness and fatherly love? To what degree is that real to you right now?
>
> Are you having any particular seasons of sweet delight in God? Do you really sense his presence in your life, sense him giving you his love?
>
> Have you been finding Scripture to be alive and active? Instead of just being a book, do you feel like Scripture is coming after you?
>
> Are you finding certain biblical promises extremely precious and encouraging? Which ones?
>
> Are you finding God calling you or challenging you to something through the Word? In what ways?
>
> Are you finding God's grace more glorious and moving now than you have in the past? Are you conscious of a growing sense of the evil of your heart, and in response, a growing dependence on and grasp of the preciousness of the mercy of God?[7]

The purpose of Keller's questions is not to induce guilt or divide any congregation into good guys and bad guys. The goal is reflected in Lamentations 3:40—"Let us examine our ways and test them, and let us return to the LORD."

Dr. Keller's questions are self-diagnostic and would be thought-provoking tools for journaling or reviewing in a small group setting or one-on-one with a mentor.

Actually, this exercise has value for each of us. For longtime believers, new converts, backsliders, those who may be unsure of where they stand in God's family, and perhaps even seekers and skeptics, because God loves them too! He is constantly drawing all people to himself. As Hebrews 3:15 implores, "Today, if you hear his voice, do not harden your hearts."

One other thought on this critical and possibly divisive topic. If you skipped over those questions because you are supremely confident you have your act together, then I beg you to walk carefully. It's not uncommon for us to look at the obvious sin in the lives of others while denying where we fall short of God's best for our own lives. We need to take to heart Matthew 7:5: "You hypocrite, first take the plank out of your own eye, and then you will see clearly to remove the speck from your brother's eye."

Checking the List

Are you a nominal Christian? Does that question sound a little harsh coming from an author who continues to work on his own relationship with God? Well, wouldn't you like to know where you stand sooner rather than later? Consider it a top priority for your to-do list.

✓ *Do some spiritual self-diagnosis.*

Get a Posse

If I'm going to drag myself out of bed and show up for a seven a.m. meeting, I'm going to make sure that time is not wasted. Just ask Bob, Dennis, Dick, Gary, Jack, John, John, Larry, Mitch, Peter, Rob, Steve, and Tom. They know I love to stir up discussion and make them think. And make myself think.

I'm talking about the guys in my small group with whom I've been meeting upstairs at Graham's 318 Coffeehouse, a local independent shop in Geneva, Illinois, for almost a decade. I've been in three other small groups over the years, and I'm fortunate that all of them have seemed to match my spiritual and emotional needs during those seasons of my life.

My initial small group, led by Mike Penny, got me regularly opening the Bible for the first time to apply it to my life. My next group, led by Mark Salzmann, forced me to deal with some personal issues that needed attention. Dave George led a group of dads that helped me identify my personal ministry. I was raising teens when most of the group was dealing with younger kids and toddlers, and I realized I had quite a bit of practical fathering experience worth sharing.

In this season of life, as Denny O'Malley leads, our group gets right down to business and spends an entire hour and a half digging through a few passages of Scripture. And it's a blast. Really. We do have serious discussions on dogma and theology, but it's amazing how often some obscure Bible passage relates to a news event, political scandal, or personal dilemma one of us is experiencing. And we laugh. A lot.

My past thirty years in four different small groups underscores the truth of Hebrews 10:24-25: "Let us consider how to stir up one another to love and good works, not neglecting to meet together, as is the habit of some, but encouraging one another, and all the more as you see the Day drawing near" (ESV).

The books we've read together are not surprising. We've talked about identifying love languages, living purpose-driven lives, and building a case for Christ. We've scribbled our way through topical study guides and had some pretty deep discussions on books like C.S. Lewis's *The Screwtape Letters*. In some of our most revealing sessions, we have simply used our study Bibles to walk through different books of the Bible. We take a chapter a week, and everyone gets a chance to pose a question or share an insight. Between studies—every four weeks or so—we set aside a morning to go around the table with prayer requests.

It's not difficult or mysterious. But it is powerful. Our fast-paced world doesn't typically allow for a group of men or women to slow down for ninety minutes to talk about stuff that really matters. The best thing about my Friday mornings is that I find myself thinking about issues and people outside my own little world. It makes me less selfish. I actually care about these guys!

All of this to say, put "small group" on your to-do list. Join one or start one. Hey, if I can drag my lazy self out of bed at six thirty most Fridays, so can you. Or meet in the evening if you prefer.

Don't worry if you travel and might miss a few gatherings. Don't worry if you're shy. Don't worry if you're not a spiritual giant. It's actually advantageous if the members are not all the same age, same income, or same level of spiritual maturity. Jesus had a small group that included guys who fished, collected taxes, and showed every kind of emotion, including fear, doubt, anger, love, greed, and courage. You should expect the same kind of diversity and intellectual stimulation from your group.

Over the decades, I've had the privilege to see God work in the lives of some pretty great guys. As a group, we've prayed our kids through college decisions, addictions, infertility, unplanned pregnancies, lost jobs, new jobs, and weddings. We've celebrated babies, grandbabies, foster babies, and adoptions. Dave suddenly got laid off but ended up with a job closer to home with a bigger, better company. Tom left the corporate world and dedicated himself to ministry. Jay had a few books published. Terry got sober. And four guys beat cancer. Gentlemen, I salute you all.

Checking the List

It's about doing life together. Holding each other accountable. Lifting each other up. Knowing that other men and women are asking the same questions as you. And finding answers together. Eternal answers.

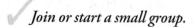 *Join or start a small group.*

Draw in the Sand

In a recent dialogue with David Taylor, a professor at Fuller Theological Seminary, Bono was asked to identify what he has learned about God from reading the Psalms. "He listens," Bono said. The lead singer of the legendary band U2 went on to admit, "I don't listen enough."[8]

Bono then referenced a memorable scene from John, chapter 8, as an example of Jesus really listening. In the temple courts, people had gathered to hear Jesus teach. A group of Pharisees interrupt, bringing in a woman caught in adultery to see if they can trick Jesus into contradicting the law. But Jesus turns the tables on them by letting his silence do most of the speaking.

> They put her in front of the crowd. "Teacher," they said to Jesus, "this woman was caught in the act of adultery. The law of Moses says to stone her. What do you say?"
>
> They were trying to trap him into saying something they could use against him, but Jesus stooped down and wrote in the dust with his finger. They kept demanding an answer, so he stood up again and said, "All right, but let the one who has never sinned throw the first stone!" Then he stooped down again and wrote in the dust.
>
> When the accusers heard this, they slipped away one by one,

beginning with the oldest, until only Jesus was left in the middle of the crowd with the woman. Then Jesus stood up again and said to the woman, "Where are your accusers? Didn't even one of them condemn you?"

"No, Lord," she said.

And Jesus said, "Neither do I. Go and sin no more" (John 8:3-11 NLT).

What was Jesus tracing in the sand? The sins of the accusers? Their names? The exact wording of the Old Testament law? Perhaps he created a temporary drawing in the dust that evoked a deeper truth about sin, guilt, and humanity's need for grace. Thoughtful art—including subway graffiti, your favorite U2 anthem, or Michelangelo's *David*—can lead people to stop, listen, and choose wisely.

In the interview, Bono calls the account of Jesus writing in the dust "a rich moment." He encourages pastors to "look for the drawing in the sand" and calls young artists to "draw in the sand." He explains, "I say this because it's my own aspiration to listen more, to be silent more. To both draw in the sand more and to look for the drawing in the sand more."

Jesus did not fall into the scribes' and Pharisees' trap. His strategy is one you and I can use. He listened, carefully measured his words, spoke a single thought-provoking sentence, and gave his audience time to think it through. In any kind of debate, the person who talks the longest and loudest often loses. Blowhards may generate more sound-bites and even get more cheers from the crowd, but their words are hollow and miss the mark. Those who take in all the facts, consider what's best for all involved, and offer a reasoned response almost always get their point across more effectively.

Worth noting, the Bible translation above includes an exclamation mark at the end of Jesus's single statement to his accusers, but I don't think he would have been emphatic with his words. I imagine Jesus using a prudent, rational, deliberate tone. Don't you?

Also worth noting, Jesus chose not to condemn the woman for her adultery. But he also didn't ignore what she had done. With clarity, Jesus did say, "Go and sin no more." If the Pharisees' trap had led to great shouting and accusing, that simple and valuable truth may have never been spoken to the woman.

So what does all this mean for your to-do list from God? It looks like this chapter may offer you five options from which to choose: Listen more. Consider your words. Draw in the sand. Look for the drawing in the sand. Go and sin no more.

Did you choose one? I hope so. When you read this book again next year, maybe you'll choose a different item for your to-do list.

Checking the List

Poise is such a valuable and rare commodity. Composure and discretion allow us to take time before we react. We should balance our lives so we're not in a constant state of panic or exasperation. When pharisaical thoughts creep in, we may be tempted to erupt and accuse. But what if we leaned over and traced in the dust?

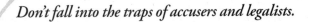 *Don't fall into the traps of accusers and legalists.*

Laugh

Doctors, dating experts, and the Bible all say that laughing should be on your to-list. You have your own sense of humor, and it may take some self-analysis to decipher what pushes your giggle button. But for your health, love life, and faith, laugh-inducing tactics are worth pursuing on a regular basis. I'm quite serious.

The Mayo Foundation for Medical Education and Research reports that laughing lightens your load, and not just mentally. It actually induces physical changes in your body. That includes enhancing your intake of oxygen-rich air, increasing the endorphins released by your brain, and stimulating your heart, lungs, and muscles. According to the doctors at the Mayo Clinic, laughter relieves stress, lessens depression, soothes tension, improves your immune system, and even causes your body to produce its own painkillers.[9]

When it comes to dating...in a study released by eHarmony, researchers in London and Oxford found that laughter on dates may help couples to let down their guard and share more personal information. The release of endorphins helps create social bonds more quickly.[10]

The Bible confirms the benefits of keeping a sunny disposition. Solomon wrote, "A joyful heart is good medicine, but a crushed spirit dries up the bones" (Proverbs 17:22 ESV). Laughter is also contagious.

Proverbs 15:13 encourages you to spread joy: "A happy heart makes the face cheerful."

Maybe one of the best reasons to laugh is that Satan hates it. His goal is to fill your life with despair and to ransack your joy. John 10:10 says, "The thief comes only to steal and kill and destroy; I have come that they may have life, and have it to the full."

We can laugh at Satan with joy and confidence because he has already been defeated. Martin Luther said, "The best way to drive out the devil, if he will not yield to texts of Scripture, is to jeer and flout him, for he cannot bear scorn."

Even God laughs at evil because he sees the bigger picture. "The wicked plot against the godly; they snarl at them in defiance. But the Lord just laughs, for he sees their day of judgment coming" (Psalm 37:12-13 NLT).

So actively pursue people and resources that make you laugh. Certain friends. Comedians. Authors. Comic strips. Tasteful sitcoms and websites. Classic movies. Your kids. Your nieces and nephews. Your siblings. Grandkids.

The best I can do right now is share a few of my favorite jokes. If you don't laugh, I apologize. But you can't say I didn't try.

Sound the Alarm

A woman frantically calls the fire department to report a fire in her neighborhood. The dispatcher asks, "Well, lady, how do we get there?" Confused, she replies, "Don't you still have those big red trucks?"

Emojis Are Easier

A mom sends a text to her son. "Hi, Son. What do IDK, ILY, GTG, and TTYL mean?" He texts back, "I don't know. I love you. Got to go. Talk to you later." The mom responds, "It's okay. I thought you'd know. I'll ask your sister."

Double Up

A linguistics professor tells the class, "In English, a double negative forms a positive. However, in some languages, such as Russian, a double negative remains a negative. But there isn't a single language, not one, in which a double positive can express a negative." A voice from the back of the room calls out, "Yeah, right."

Beethoven's Grave

A week after Beethoven's death, the cemetery caretaker hears strange rustling sounds coming from the grave site and sends for the grave digger. After finally digging down six feet, the grave digger pries the lid off the casket and peeks in to see Beethoven erasing sheets of music. The gravedigger looks up at the caretaker and says, "Just as I thought. He's decomposing."

Animal Crackers

A mom walks into the kitchen and sees her daughter has dumped a whole box of animal crackers onto the counter. She says, "What are you doing? You really should eat one at a time." The little girl says, "But, Mom, the box says, 'Do not eat if the seal is broken.' And I can't find the seal."

Again, I do apologize. If you can do better, send me your best short, clean jokes. You can find me at jaypayleitner.com.

Checking the List

Ecclesiastes 3:2-4 confirms there is "a time to plant and a time to uproot, a time to kill and a time to heal, a time to tear down and a time to build, time to weep and a time to laugh, a time to mourn and a time to dance."

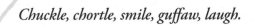 *Chuckle, chortle, smile, guffaw, laugh.*

Face Your Fears

When I was seven, I was deathly afraid of the basement. It was home to our furnace, a huge fire-belching monster with unwieldly asbestos-covered arms that hissed, moaned, and roared through three of the four seasons. When my mom or dad sent me downstairs to grab a screwdriver or a basket of laundry, I would tiptoe down and race back up. It gave me the willies. (Do people still get the willies?)

When I was eight, my dad (without asking my opinion) portioned off a section of that basement and built some bunkbeds into the corner. That was the new bedroom for my brother and me. This wasn't a case of child abuse. My parents weren't coercing me to face my fears. No one in my family even knew I was afraid of the basement.

It turned out to be a good thing. Eight-year-olds who are loved and secure are pretty resilient creatures. In those basement bunk beds, Mark and I found a new freedom to lay awake and talk. Plotting mischief and planning bike hikes. Dreaming dreams and facing fears. The fierce-looking furnace just around the corner no longer held power over me.

So, what are you afraid of? Is liberating yourself of a certain fear something you can check off your to-do list? It may not be easy, but if eight-year-old Jay can overcome the willies, so can you. For sure, some phobias can be paralyzing and have a legitimate basis. But much of the time, with a bit of common sense and grit, you can overcome those fears.

Give yourself a little credit and a fighting chance. Especially if someone you love has led you to a situation that calls for you to muster up a new dose of courage. I faced another fear just this year. My grandson's fourth birthday party was held at the local park district nature center. When the animal wrangler offered, I surprised myself by voluntarily carrying around a six-foot python for several minutes. I figured if a bunch of preschoolers could touch a snake, so could I.

Really, the goal is not to deny your fears, but to work around them. When my kids were younger, one of them was afraid of lightning, and another was afraid of spiders. They didn't stay locked shivering in their room, so these were never paralyzing problems. My wife, Rita, has a bit of acrophobia, so I guess I won't be taking her mountain climbing anytime soon.

To be clear, I would never just say to you or anyone, "Get over it." And even though I know quoting Scripture won't magically make you fearless, it's never a bad place to turn.

- "The LORD himself goes before you and will be with you; he will never leave you nor forsake you. Do not be afraid; do not be discouraged" (Deuteronomy 31:8).

- "Peace I leave with you; my peace I give you. I do not give to you as the world gives. Do not let your hearts be troubled and do not be afraid" (John 14:27).

Confirming…that's a direct order from both the Old and New Testament—"Do not be afraid."

All in all, let's not forget that fear can be a healthy emotion. We want small children to be a little afraid of crossing the street alone, eating mushrooms from the backyard, and petting strange dogs. Even for grown-ups, a little fear can lead us to be more careful and better prepared. When we're afraid, we might reach out to others for help or find new courage or creativity as we stand up to our phobias.

Finally, it's worth noting that even humorist Dave Barry confirms that fear is nothing to be ashamed of. "All of us are born with a set of instinctive fears—of falling, of the dark, of lobsters, of falling on lobsters in the dark, of speaking before a Rotary Club, and of the words 'Some assembly required.'"

Checking the List

Some fears are just silly. Some are legitimate. All are temporary. They will not follow us into eternity. The best option is to accept Jesus's perfect love because "Perfect love casts out fear" (1 John 4:18 NASB).

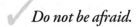 *Do not be afraid.*

Be like Simon

Imagine Simon of Cyrene. In Jerusalem for Passover, his mind is back home. He has been gone for weeks, and surely his boys Alex and Rufus are up to their old tricks. He's really just passing through. On this Friday evening, he would rather have been home reading the papyrus and watching a little gladiator practice from his balcony. He notices a bit of commotion near the city gate and wonders, *What's going on?*

Then his day gets serious. Simon is swept up in a crowd of onlookers near a rocky pathway through Jerusalem. A convicted blasphemer stumbles through the final hours of his life, forced by Roman soldiers to carry his own instrument of death. From onlookers, Simon learns that Pilate sentenced the man in his early thirties to be crucified on Golgotha, a hill just outside of town. Drawing closer to the scene, Simon makes eye contact with the cross carrier, who wears an expression that can only described as a fusion of fear, determination, and compassion. *Who is this man?* Weakened and bleeding profusely from a recent severe scourging, the man stumbles. *There's no way he can make it up this steep path.*

With no warning, a guard in full armor grabs Simon's shoulder and shoves him in the path of the criminal. *What now? What have I done?* Simon hears an order. Propelled by fear and his own unexpected compassion, he obeys. With a grunt, he hoists the heavy crossbeam onto his own back. *How has this wounded man carried this burden?* Relieved of the oppressive weight, Jesus of Nazareth takes a full breath into his lungs and stands tall for just a moment. He sees faces. He hears the weeping and the jeers. He feels it all. And then he turns and leads Simon toward Golgotha, the Place of the Skull.

Simon of Cyrene is mentioned only three times in the Bible. The gospels of Matthew, Mark, and Luke barely describe the scene. We really don't know why Simon is in Jerusalem. Or whether he stayed to watch the crucifixion…or the resurrection.

But we do know he carried the cross.

For centuries, that phrase has been used to describe the burdens people take on. We say things like "I guess raising an unruly teenager is my cross to bear." Or "My illness is a cross I'll have to carry." Or you might imagine some linebacker saying, "Coach, you can count on me to lead this football team. I'll carry that cross."

But it's more than that. For a full explanation, all we have to do is turn to Matthew 16:24-25. Days or perhaps months before his death on the cross, Jesus challenges his disciples, "Whoever wants to be my disciple must deny themselves and take up their cross and follow me. For whoever wants to save their life will lose it, but whoever loses their life for me will find it."

That's pretty clear. This is not about taking one for the team or putting up with an inconvenience for a while. It's about each of us giving up our life for Jesus because he gave up his life for us. That's a pretty good trade.

I have to assume Simon traveled 900 miles back to his family in Cyrene (now Libya) a changed man. He didn't know why he was recruited, but he got the job done. You can't have that kind of intimate interaction with the Son of Man without coming away a different person. We don't really know Simon's emotional response to his role as cross carrier. Initially he might have been reluctant or angry. But when it comes down to it, Simon was the only person besides Jesus to actually carry that now-famous and ubiquitous cross.

Are you jealous? I am a bit. I'd like to think I would have stepped up, lifted that beam, and carried it as far as Jesus wanted. I don't know if I could have stayed and watched the nails enter his hands and feet. It's not pleasant to even think about. Especially since it was my sin that put Jesus on that cross.

Checking the List

The Bible and the life of Christ are not fiction. We should never forget that we're talking about historic events with real people who had real hopes and fears. The culture has changed, but we are not really that different from people like Simon of Cyrene, Peter, Mary Magdalene, Pontius Pilate, and the centurion standing guard at the foot of the cross who witnessed Jesus's death, saw the earthquake, and said, "Surely he was the Son of God!"

✓ *Carry the cross.*

43

Forgive That Person

In previous chapters we've talked about coming before God and asking for forgiveness. That's a critical item for most to-do lists. Reaching that moment of brokenness—realizing your need for a Savior and repenting of your sins—is actually a wonderful thing. Really.

You come to realize you can't possibly do life right until that happens. When all the pieces fall into place and you really understand how grace works, the final decision to seek God's grace makes perfect sense. You might even call it obvious and easy.

On the other hand...what's not easy is forgiving that one person who really did some serious damage to you a while back.

Sorry to bring that episode to mind, but it's never really far away, is it? You were hurt emotionally, physically, spiritually, financially, relationally, or all of the above. And the offending individual was not in a hurry to apologize. Maybe they didn't know what they did. Maybe they don't care. Maybe they're suffering in their own world of hurt. You can't read their mind.

Unless God intervenes, there's not much chance they are going to come to you with sincere regrets. Unfortunately, there are many reasons people *don't* apologize. They live in denial and don't want to feel guilt or shame. They fear legal repercussions for their actions. They're afraid admitting their mistake will encourage you or others to pile on with more accusations. They think apologies are a sign of weakness.

So what do you do? First, stop waiting for their apology. Second, if you think they might listen, there is a biblical approach spelled out in Matthew 18:15-17.

> If your brother or sister sins, go and point out their fault, just between the two of you. If they listen to you, you have won them over. But if they will not listen, take one or two others along, so that "every matter may be established by the testimony of two or three witnesses." If they still refuse to listen, tell it to the church; and if they refuse to listen even to the church, treat them as you would a pagan or a tax collector.

That seems more than fair. You give them three chances and then treat them as someone not to be trusted. But if ever they do show genuine remorse, be ready to accept their apology. Luke 17:3 confirms, "If your brother or sister sins against you, rebuke them; and if they repent, forgive them."

But what if you simply cannot be in the same room with the offending scoundrel? Either they're dead, dangerous, or unavailable. There are still biblical strategies for shaking this burden from your heart and mind. Stop hoping for any kind of reconciliation—which is a two-way alliance. Instead, settle for the courageous act of one-way forgiveness. That's just you saying, "God, I'm not going to let this drag me down anymore. I'm choosing right now to give this burden to you."

Jesus modeled one-way forgiveness on the cross. He never had a conversation with those who scourged him, mocked him, or nailed his feet and hands. He never confronted them, and they never hinted at an apology. But from his vantage point on the cross, he expressed supernatural love. "Jesus said, 'Father, forgive them, for they do not know what they are doing'" (Luke 23:34).

That's the consummate example of the forgiving spirit that Jesus describes in a conversation with Peter in Matthew 18:21:

> Peter came to Jesus and asked, "Lord, how many times shall I forgive my brother or sister who sins against me? Up to seven times?"
>
> Jesus answered, "I tell you, not seven times, but seventy-seven times."

You may think that most long-term grudges involve strangers, business associates, former friends, or nasty people with whom you happened to cross paths. But actually, the people who hurt you most often are probably the people with whom you spend the most time and who know exactly how to push your buttons—your family.

Come to think of it, except in cases of severe trauma, forgiving strangers is easy. You can do it without confronting them. Forgiving members of your own family is a little tougher. That includes your teenager who reacted sarcastically to your question. Your sibling who wouldn't take your side in a dispute. Your spouse who overreacted to a minor offense and won't let it go.

There may be four or five things to remember with family squabbles. First, the goal is not just forgiveness; it's true reconciliation. Second, there's probably some minor miscommunication or misunderstanding involved that got blown out of proportion. Which means it's often helpful to be the bigger person and give your family member the benefit of the doubt.

Third, if you're holding something against them, there's a good chance they're holding something against you, and you may want to consider how *you* contributed to the kerfuffle. Fourth, the longer it goes, the bigger it will become as other family members take sides.

Finally, you need to get this resolved because according to Mark 11:25, neither of you can get right with God until you get right with each other. That verse reads, "Whenever you stand praying, forgive, if you have anything against anyone, so that your Father also who is in heaven may forgive you your trespasses" (ESV).

So check your to-do list in this regard. The process of giving and receiving forgiveness may not be easy, but it almost always has a happy ending. Family members experiencing an emotional reconciliation often find themselves in a new season of rewarding relationship with each other and with God.

Checking the List

In many cases, forgiving someone does not mean you have to let them back into your life. Over time, reconciliation may or may not take place. Still, once you make the decision to forgive, you should expect to experience a sense of relief that the burden is gone.

 Give that bitterness to God.

Reset Your Car Radio

I respect the podcast revolution. I've even partially succumbed to it.
On road trips I have several favorites. But there's still something
serendipitous about good old-fashioned radio. Flip the dial, and you
never know what might pop on. And truthfully, it's in my blood.

By trade, I'm a radio producer. For more than 20 years, most of my
time was spent as a freelancer producing radio spots, specials, short
features, interview programs, and fundraising campaigns for some
of the country's most prominent ministries and Christian publishers. That includes weekly radio with Josh McDowell and annual fun-
draisers with Chuck Colson for the Prison Fellowship Project Angel
Tree campaign.

I cowrote more than four thousand scripts for *Today's Father*, a short
feature for the National Center for Fathering. On behalf of the Voice of
the Martyrs, I recorded scores of programs with TobyMac and Michael
Tait for *Jesus Freaks Radio*. I also launched radio features for the Heri-
tage Foundation, Bible League, and the Susan B. Anthony List. Other
past clients include the Salvation Army, Red Cross, Food for the Hungry, Mercy Corps, and Awana.

All of the above requires people talking into microphones saying
things that are worth saying. I love and appreciate good talk radio.

On a good talk station, you can expect to find breaking news stories, sports updates, weather alerts, some cheerful banter, movie reviews, scrappy interviews, healthy debates providing both sides of controversial issues, an occasional goofy story, and a few voices you can trust. It adds up to listeners who are culturally aware. For years, I have counted on talk radio to be a loyal and engaging resource that would make me think, smile, and listen to news I could use.

But not anymore. Talk radio is now just too painful. It's mostly nonstop bashing, belittling, whining, falsifying, spinning, twisting, and making you wish you weren't listening. So I don't.

In recent days, I've locked my Chicago-area dial to WBGL FM 104.7 for a steady stream of contemporary Christian music. Which leaves me humming some uplifting tunes with uplifting lyrics for much of the day.

I do realize this is a phase. Probably just a short season of rebellion against trashy talk radio. I fully expect to explore other options—which is my history.

I know that someday soon I'll return to the soul-satisfying diet of my local Moody radio station. The Chicago flagship, 90.1 FM, has some music along with the familiar voices of quite a few friends with whom I've worked over the years: Chris Fabry, Mike Kellogg, Jon Gauger, Anita Lustrea, Melinda Schmidt. Not to mention other national colleagues like Steve Brown, Jim Daly, and Tony Evans.

Then, for some reason I'll tune into the local progressive talk station to see what they're saying. That only lasts a couple car trips before I want to pull my hair out. What's left of it anyway.

NPR is a great listen on weekends, especially with *This American Life*, *Wait Wait…Don't Tell Me*, and *The Moth Radio Hour*.

Of course, I've got buttons for a couple of classic rock stations when I need a fix of the Beatles, Elton, Chicago, the Beach Boys, and wimpy hits from the '70s. I will also flip to stations that play current hits from artists whose names I can't keep straight. I even have a country station on my console.

The desperate cacophony of talk radio may settle down. But for sure, the noise of the world will continue to be a drag. So there's a good chance I'll always find my way back to stations that have an authentic biblical message. Some talk. Some preaching. Some music.

I recommend you try it. Conversely, I fully expect to continue my transition to listening to more podcasts. The trouble there, of course, is that it's tempting to download only podcasters with whom you agree. I think it's critical to take in opposing and diverse viewpoints once in a while. That's why, when you're driving, it's wise sometimes to let whoever is sitting shotgun choose the station.

Bottom line. I believe good Christian radio offers a little taste of what it might be like in heaven. Especially if you let the music, heartfelt messages, and respect for truth sink in.

In other words, "Let the message of Christ dwell among you richly as you teach and admonish one another with all wisdom through psalms, hymns, and songs from the Spirit, singing to God with gratitude in your hearts" (Colossian 3:16).

Checking the List

Christian media is not meant to take you away from the world. Instead, use the teaching, lyrics, and thoughtful discussion to equip you to enter the world and be salt and light. Soon you'll be humming with confidence and sharing a message worth passing on to others.

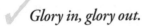 *Glory in, glory out.*

Pretend

I just finished "reading" a delightful board book with my grand-daughter. Reese is one and a half years old and smiles a mile when Chief—that's me—enters the room. The beloved book, *First Words*, is 20 pages with 20 single photos and 20 single-word descriptions: girl, boy, socks, shoes, coat, cup, boat, car, truck, train, airplane, teddy, orange, apple, banana, leaf, flower, cat, duck, fish.

Reesie does an entertaining and excellent job quacking at the duck and meowing at the kitty, but when we turn to the page with fruit, she leans into the picture and pretends to eat the orange or the apple. "Nom nom nom nom!"

Does Reesie really think it's a delicious and juicy apple or orange? Of course not! And I also don't worry that she believes photos are edible. My granddaughter and a million other kids who read these books are *pretending*. It's a good thing when kids imagine the existence of a giant red dog, talking train engine, taco-eating dragons, and six-foot cat in a hat.

Frankly, most grown-ups need to spend a little more time in the land of make-believe. Imagination is a valuable skill, a muscle we need to exercise.

If you've been reading these chapters sequentially, this author has already invited you to imagine all kinds of things, including reading your father's boyhood journal, walking through your childhood home, and reliving the historic moment when Simon of Cyrene helped Jesus carry the cross.

Pretending comes in handy when you're trying to fake interest in your boss's paperclip collection. Also, I totally encourage couples to take their lunch out on the patio and pretend to be at a Parisian café. Pretending you're having a good time at a social gathering is sometimes the wise choice—especially when in-laws are involved.

Imagination lays the groundwork for all human endeavors. From inventing the printing press to climbing Mount Everest to writing *Hamilton*. Guttenberg, Hillary, and Miranda had to imagine it before they did it.

When Jesus delivers his memorable parables, he invites us to *imagine* a young man insisting on an early inheritance and spending it foolishly, or a traveler being robbed by bandits and cared for by a Samaritan stranger.

It certainly requires imagination to consider what heaven might be like. In Revelation 21:21, the Bible uses human terms to describe heaven: "The twelve gates were twelve pearls, each made of a single pearl. The great street of the city was of gold, as pure as transparent glass." We get a much better picture if we close our eyes and just imagine the most beautifully satisfying place our mind can create. Still, even that falls short. In 1 Corinthians 2:9 we read, "No eye has seen, no ear has heard, and no mind has imagined what God has prepared for those who love him" (NLT).

Finally, take it from me, pretending is a valuable skill for parents and grandparents. Pretending you don't see a three-year-old hiding behind a skinny sapling is the funniest thing in the world. Except maybe for talking into a banana as if it were a phone, which is even funnier. When you're raising a fashion-forward teenager, pretending you appreciate the latest fashion trends is a useful skill. When you drop off your college student, you may feel as if you have to pretend not to be overcome with emotion. But really, it's okay to sniff back some tears.

So let's pretend more. And use our imaginations. And flex our creative muscles to envision how we might impact the world for the glory of God.

Checking the List

Most of us could be a little more childlike. Of course, if you're one of those adults who already spend a lot of time in fantasyland, then maybe you need to do a 180-degree turn and walk in reality for a while.

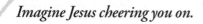 *Imagine Jesus cheering you on.*

Delay Gratification

You may already know about the Stanford Marshmallow Test, a study from the late 1960s researching humans' potential to delay gratification. Simply stated, children age four to six were given a choice of one marshmallow now or two marshmallows if they waited fifteen minutes. The video of these kids left in a room by themselves with that single tantalizing treat is quite amusing. Some kids snarfed the marshmallow as soon as the adult researcher left the room. Most attempted to distract themselves from the temptation—covering their faces, grimacing, talking to themselves, turning away in their chair, sniffing or petting the marshmallow, playing with their own hair, fingers, or nose, and so on. About one-third of the children successfully deferred gratification long enough to earn the second treat.

Several variables were considered, and the actual research was more complicated than stated here, but you get the point. It's worth noting that a follow-up study years later found that the children who were patient enough to earn a second marshmallow tended to score higher on SAT scores as teenagers.

The application of delayed gratification extends far beyond sugary treats. And there's a good chance you are facing some decisions now that will reap rewards in the future—or not, depending on what choice you make today. Here are just a few real-life examples of delayed gratification.

Staying in school. Sure, you're tired of books and teachers' dirty looks. But you know that degree is going to be a significant benefit when you go job hunting.

Saving up and paying cash. If you buy something on credit now and make minimum payments, you could easily spend two or three times as much on that car, vacation, leather couch, and so on. Plus, because of the anticipation and the satisfaction of knowing the item is already paid for, whatever you buy will mean so much more if you wait and pay cash.

Playing with toddlers. Do you remember anything before you were three years old? Probably not. So why should a parent bother spending time with a baby or toddler? They won't remember it anyway, right? I hope you don't take that reasoning seriously, because those early years are critical for building trust, gaining self-confidence, establishing life-long habits, and learning how to give love and receive love.

Not throwing curve balls before muscle maturity. There are many ways young athletes push themselves too hard too soon, leading to burnout and injuries. In baseball, Little League pitchers should stick to fastballs and change-ups. Otherwise, repetitive stress will damage tendons, ligaments, and muscles in the elbows and shoulders of their throwing arm. In their teens, when actual scouts are watching, they won't be able to perform.

Avoiding gambling. The Bible promises, "Greedy people try to get rich quick but don't realize they're headed for poverty" (Proverbs 28:22 NLT). That's not really a surprise, is it? Who do you think pays for all those glitzy casinos? Why do so many lottery winners end up destitute and miserable? You gamble, you lose.

Maintaining virginity. For several years, the idea of saving yourself for your wedding night was mocked. In many circles now, sexual purity before marriage is once again a reasonable expectation. The many physical, spiritual, psychological, economic, and social benefits are well documented.

Pausing before giving in to the latest technology. Sure it's fun to be the first with the hottest product, but early adopters take all kinds of risks. Price tags are higher. Bugs are not worked out. And you waste a lot of time in line at the Apple store or showing off your new toy. (Which is obsolete in six months anyway.)

Planting a tree. Trust me, there are few things in life more satisfying than sitting in the shade of a maple tree you planted twenty years earlier. Now that's delayed gratification!

Should "have more patience" or "delay gratification" be on your to-do list? Maybe we could turn that idea into something that sounds more proactive, such as "persevere" or "keep doing good." Galatians 6:9 (NLT) promises, "Let's not get tired of doing what is good. At just the right time we will reap a harvest of blessing if we don't give up."

Checking the List

In many cases, it really is okay to eat the single marshmallow or buy the latest gadget. Just realize you may be sacrificing some benefit or reward down the road. When in doubt, pause. Delay most gratifications...maybe for quite a while.

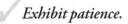 *Exhibit patience.*

47

Think and Do

There's a pseudo-religious movement making its way around the world called the "law of attraction." It was popularized in the book by Rhonda Byrne titled *The Secret*. Her claim was that life can be perfect if we simply visualize success or think good thoughts. She writes, "If you think about what you want in your mind, and make that your dominant thought, you *will* bring it into your life."[11]

Byrne points out that she didn't invent the concept. Some 75 years ago, motivational speaker Robert Collier claimed, "See the things that you want as already yours. Know that they will come to you at need. Then let them come."[12]

Do those claims sound a bit frightening to you? They should. Alarm bells should be going off in your head.

Simple common sense tells us imagining a situation does not guarantee it does or will exist. Thinking skinny won't transform cheeseburgers and éclairs into health food. A college student who parties the entire semester and skips classes cannot generate passing grades by simply imagining his assignments have been completed. Good thoughts may bring comfort to your uncle in his time of crisis, but his cancer may or may not go into remission.

Let me be clear. The law of attraction has nothing to do with prayer. It's actually the opposite. Prayer works because it's all about submitting to the will of the Creator of the universe. When we surrender our trust in prayer, he weaves our sincere requests into his eternal plan. Conversely, the law of attraction describes a selfish human visualizing his or her own narcissistic desires.

Let me also confirm the life-sustaining value of optimism and hope. Hope is an essential ingredient of the Christian life. Near the end of his letter to the Romans, Paul writes, "May the God of hope fill you with all joy and peace as you trust in him, so that you may overflow with hope by the power of the Holy Spirit" (Romans 15:13). Positive thinking is a wonderful first step, but we should never confuse it with the end of the journey.

I'm equally in favor of imagination and creativity. Every invention, painting, fictional character, dance step, sculpture, or equation was imagined before it was created. Successful athletes visualize their footwork, swing, shot, dive, or stance in their mind before performing. They're imagining the culmination of all their hard work. God designed the mind and body to work together.

Are you beginning to see how the law of attraction is actually the antithesis of dreaming big dreams and doing great deeds? Thinking does not equate to doing. We should never expect or desire to bypass or trivialize the quest for excellence. There's great joy in the journey. Heroes are made, not wished into existence.

Perhaps the worst repercussion of *The Secret* and books like it are how they provide false hope for people who need real hope. How many individuals have been duped into ignoring the value of working hard and risking all and have never even given themselves the chance for victory?

People in search of meaning for their lives don't need to envision themselves surrounded by easily acquired riches. That's passive. That's lazy. On our own, each of us needs to actively approach the throne of God and seek to reflect his character in our lives. That's the secret we need to shout from the rooftop. That's the secret to an abundant, satisfying, all-your-needs-met life.

The final word on the topic comes in the familiar words of Matthew 6:33: "Seek the Kingdom of God above all else, and live righteously, and he will give you everything you need" (NLT).

Checking the List

Optimism, imagination, prayer, and hope are not passive activities. They fully engage our entire body and soul. They don't just lead to action, they *are* action.

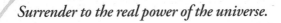 *Surrender to the real power of the universe.*

48

Be an Emcee

In his renowned blog, Victor Saad, founder of Experience Institute, applauds the way a great emcee can have a profound impact on an event featuring speakers, musicians, performers, and so on. Specifically, how an engaging and well-prepared emcee will set the stage for each act.

> They research everything about the event. They know the performers, the venue, the city, and specifics about the audience. They take all of that knowledge and use it to build excitement and anticipation for each part of the event.

> A great emcee can reference some of the nuances of each act—how the performer is going to use a certain instrument, or where the act originated, or how special it is that they are here for this occasion.

> Then, they'll rile up the crowd.[13]

Saad describes the power an emcee has to amplify energy with an audience and help launch performers into their own magical moment on stage. Conversely, if the emcee fails to do the job, performers may forfeit their opportunity to touch the audience before they even walk on stage.

Then in a twist of inspiration, Saad reminds us that you and I have that same power to help those around us launch their own life performances. He writes, "Everyone around you needs an emcee."

It's a stunning analogy. And putting this idea into action is worthy of your to-do list. In all likelihood, there are more than a dozen people in your circle of influence who are on the edge of achieving their dream. They are answering God's call in their life, but they've hit a roadblock or don't have the confidence to move ahead.

You may be the right person to help them take that next step with a single word of encouragement or a practical challenge. You might remind them of how far they've come or how much the world needs to hear their story. Maybe you can introduce them to another performer who could be a partner or mentor. Maybe there's a resource or program they don't know about. Some performers, writers, artists, or speakers just need someone to listen, care, and offer a fresh perspective.

A good master of ceremonies is more than a cheerleader. He or she takes the time to uncover the strengths and weaknesses of each act. An emcee lines up the event program so that each act is well received. There are headliners and there are opening acts. Some bands can captivate an audience for more than two hours. Some should play their three best songs and get off the stage. A speaker who goes longer than forty minutes risks putting an audience to sleep. And comedians need to say goodnight *before* they run out of material. An emcee sets each act up for success.

In other words, let's help our friends, colleagues, and family members put their best foot forward. Help them shine so they can give glory back to God. That's possible only if we occasionally set aside our own agenda and make the effort to help others reach their full potential.

As Saad writes, "Because the show isn't just about you…it's about all of us."

Checking the List

You didn't sign up to be an emcee. Your own to-do list is already long. But don't pass up the opportunity to lend a hand or offer a good word. Just about the time you start helping someone else nurture their "act," don't be surprised if someone else comes along and nudges you another step toward reaching your full potential. That's how the body of Christ works best.

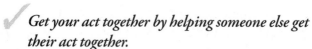 *Get your act together by helping someone else get their act together.*

Eat Healthier

Eat healthier? For sure, there are all types of slightly dangerous fad diets and fat-burning techniques that may or may not help you lose some excess weight, stay healthier, feel better, and live longer. There are also a variety of medically sound diets that would have you consuming more veggies, less fried food and sugar, some carbs, just enough protein, and lots of good old-fashioned water. But none of this is news to you.

I am no expert, but I can pass on several other commonsense tips for eating healthier. Serving smaller portions at meals. Grabbing only healthy snacks between meals. Grocery shopping when you're not hungry. Feeling the freedom to break your diet once in a while for special occasions. Making long-term lifestyle changes rather than going on fad or crash diets. Reading up on healthy life strategies without obsessing.

Also, breaking a sweat every day with a little exercise will burn calories and actually help increase your willpower.

You may even consider diets based on certain passages of the Bible written by names you recognize. *The Daniel Plan: 40 Days to a Healthier Life* by Pastor Rick Warren along with two medical doctors is getting some good reviews. Anything that might lead you to be a little more intentional about what you eat is not a bad idea.

But enough about dieting. This chapter is not really about eating healthier. I apologize if you turned to this page ready to add a bibli-cally inspired eating regimen to your to-do list. I do care about your physical well-being. But the remainder of this short chapter is about *spiritual* food.

Just as it's okay to let your tummy growl a bit sometimes, being a little spiritually hungry is also a good thing. It keeps you turning to the Bible for answers. But *starving* yourself leads to spiritual immaturity. Pastor and author John MacArthur points to the problem and the solution.

> When believers aren't growing…the root cause of their arrested development is spiritual malnourishment—their souls are starved for wholesome spiritual food. The Bible refers to itself as milk, bread, and meat, but spiritually a lot of Christians are trying to survive and thrive on candy, Cokes, and fries. They aren't growing because their diet is tragically deficient. Ironically, the solution to their problems is in the very thing they refuse to feed upon—God's Word.[14]

A hunger for God's truth is an ongoing theme in the Bible. Before beginning his earthly ministry, Jesus fasted forty days in the desert. Satan seizes the opportunity.

> The tempter came to him and said, "If you are the Son of God, tell these stones to become bread."
>
> Jesus answered, "It is written: 'Man shall not live on bread alone, but on every word that comes from the mouth of God'" (Matthew 4:3-4).

Later, after miraculously feeding the five thousand with five loaves and two small fish, Jesus explains to his disciples that more important than barley loaves or manna is the "true bread from heaven."

> "Sir," they said, "always give us this bread."
>
> Then Jesus declared, "I am the bread of life. Whoever comes

to me will never go hungry, and whoever believes in me will never be thirsty" (John 6:34-35).

The most compelling words regarding Jesus as our spiritual food came during the Last Supper. In the upper room, Jesus was about to predict Judas's betrayal and Peter's denial, and soon he would make his way to the Garden of Gethsemane. But first he confirmed what the twelve should have already known: "He took bread, gave thanks and broke it, and gave it to them, saying, 'This is my body given for you; do this in remembrance of me'" (Luke 22:19).

And you thought this chapter was going to be about your physical well-being. Next time you have the privilege of taking communion, I encourage you to make the connection between "the promises of God's Word," "the bread of life," and "the body of Christ."

Checking the List

There are many names for Jesus. Good shepherd. Light of the world. Rock. True vine. The door. The term "bread of life" expresses how he feeds our deepest hunger.

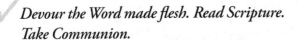 *Devour the Word made flesh. Read Scripture. Take Communion.*

Do All the Stuff the Bible Says to Do Today

There's a complaint floating around suggesting that the Bible doesn't cover everything. And there's some truth to that idea.

The microscope wasn't invented until the sixteenth century, so Scripture has no mention of amoebas or paramecium. Which means when Adam was charged with naming all the animals (Genesis 2:19-20), he obviously missed all the single-celled organisms.

Neither can you find a passage specifically mentioning electricity, glass windows, guns, cell phones, airplanes, genetic engineering, jukeboxes, nuclear energy, paper clips, satellites, or zippers. Some might say anyone who uses the Bible for instruction is lost when it comes to any inventions of the last two thousand years.

Faced with these glaring omissions, should we throw out the entire book? Well, here's the deal. There's plenty of infallible guidance in God's Word that we do know for sure. Those instructions have undeniably relevant application for today. May I suggest that if you start there and wholeheartedly pursue the instructions that are crystal clear, everything else will fall into place? Let's provide a few examples, and you can take it from there.

- *Treasure the day.* "This is the day which the LORD has made; let us rejoice and be glad in it" (Psalm 118:24 NASB).

- *Have an attitude of gratitude.* "Do not be anxious about anything, but in every situation, by prayer and petition, with thanksgiving, present your requests to God. And the peace of God, which transcends all understanding, will guard your hearts and your minds in Christ Jesus" (Philippians 4:6-7).

- *Stay heavenly minded.* "Rejoice always; pray without ceasing; in everything give thanks; for this is God's will for you in Christ Jesus" (1 Thessalonians 5:16-18 NASB).

- *Be awestruck.* "Fear the LORD your God, and live in a way that pleases him, and love him and serve him with all your heart and soul" (Deuteronomy 10:12 NLT).

- *Choose life.* "I have set before you life and death, blessings and curses. Now choose life, so that you and your children may live" (Deuteronomy 30:19).

- *Keep your heart tender.* "Today, if you hear his voice, do not harden your hearts" (Hebrews 3:15).

- *Reflect integrity.* "He has shown you, O mortal, what is good. And what does the LORD require of you? To act justly and to love mercy and to walk humbly with your God" (Micah 6:8).

- *Chill.* "Be still, and know that I am God" (Psalm 46:10).

- *Preach and teach.* "Go and make disciples of all nations, baptizing them in the name of the Father and of the Son and of the Holy Spirit, and teaching them to obey everything I have commanded you" (Matthew 28:19-20).

- *Be a team player.* "Encourage one another daily, as long as it is called 'Today,' so that none of you may be hardened by sin's deceitfulness" (Hebrews 3:13).

- *Speak truth.* "Having put away falsehood, let each one of you speak the truth with his neighbor, for we are members one of another" (Ephesians 4:25 ESV).

- *Think big picture.* "Keep his decrees and commands, which I am giving you today, so that it may go well with you and your children after you and that you may live long in the land the LORD your God gives you for all time" (Deuteronomy 4:40).

- *Make your choice.* "Choose for yourselves this day whom you will serve" (Joshua 24:15).

So that's the plan. And it's completely your choice. Pursue the activities clearly instructed in the Bible or don't. (Those listed above and hundreds more from all 66 books of the Bible.) If you do, any uncertainty that comes from confusing passages or from issues that are not explicitly addressed will melt away. God doesn't want you to stumble around desperately looking for answers. "For God is not a God of confusion but of peace" (1 Corinthians 14:33 ESV).

At this point, if you still don't have a clue about right from wrong, then search your heart. Maybe there's a reason you're anxious and angry. You have truth to seek. A mission to undertake. Proverbs 28:5 says, "Evildoers do not understand what is right, but those who seek the LORD understand it fully."

Checking the List

There's much in the Bible that takes time and wisdom to discern. But you can certainly begin by asking God to open your eyes, and then you can turn to the hundreds of straightforward, unmistakable instructive passages.

 Get going.

Pass It On

Okay, then. You've been checking off items on God's to-do list for fifty chapters. And you're feeling pretty good about yourself. You're counting the cost and eating live frogs every morning. You're praying in the moment, clearing clutter, and taking a fresh look at old Bible verses. You're even ready for Jesus to return.

Now what? It's time to take your newly embraced wisdom and pass it on. That idea might be one of the most important tenets of the faith. Truth needs to be shared. In 2 Timothy 2:1-2, Paul writes, "Be strong in the grace that is in Christ Jesus. And the things you have heard me say in the presence of many witnesses entrust to reliable people who will also be qualified to teach others."

Don't keep the good news to yourself. For sure, you have to accept Jesus as your Savior on your own. Nobody else can do that for you. But you were drawn to the faith because it was modeled by someone else. You saw how grace works and sins can be forgiven. You saw how giving glory to God gives purpose to life. You saw how the lives of those who truly follow Christ are characterized by integrity, financial security, creativity, and peace of mind. Even when a follower of Christ experienced hardship, you saw how they endured through faith.

Now it's time to pass it on. To share God's love. Once your own salvation is assured, your focus needs to turn outward. The blessings you've been given, your natural talents, and your spiritual gifts are not meant to be hoarded. Your neighbors, family, friends, work colleagues…even your enemies should be on the receiving end of those gifts. In other words, it's time to allow God's love and mercy to flow through you.

That lesson becomes quite clear when you consider two bodies of water connected by the Jordan River in the land Jesus walked. The Sea of Galilee and the Dead Sea.

The Sea of Galilee, the location of so many of Jesus's messages and miracles, is fed by spring waters and melted snow flowing from the north. At the southern end of this historic lake, the Jordan River flows out, irrigating thousands of acres of productive farmland.

Fifty miles to the south, the Jordan runs into the Dead Sea. It's one of the lowest places on Earth, thirteen hundred feet below sea level. Seven times saltier than the ocean, this lake is aptly named because it cannot sustain life.

The difference between these two lakes is obvious to any engineering geologist. The Dead Sea has no outlet. The life-giving water from the Jordan River flows in and never flows out. The Dead Sea only takes. It never gives.

We need to be like the Sea of Galilee, not the Dead Sea. To take our own abundant life promised by Jesus and pour into the lives of others with enthusiasm and consistency. But that's not the end of the transaction. The current needs to keep flowing. All believers—recent and longtime followers—have a responsibility to give and receive. Instruction and correction. Love and discipline. We need to maintain big-picture thinking while also staying aware of the small, intimate needs of those whom God puts in our path.

We're constantly teaching and learning. And learning and teaching.

So which did you do today? Hopefully a little of each. That's the overflowing life to which we have been called. Receiving abundant spiritual nourishment and wisdom so that we can pass it on to others. It's being a student and a mentor. That's how discipleship works. That's why you read books like this. That's why you're checking off items on a to-do list…not an all-done list.

In Hebrew, the word "Galilee" means wheel, circuit, or revolution. It's easy to see that life as a follower of Christ is a constant circle of love, faith, and hope that goes out to others and comes back around again and again. Blessing everyone whose life we touch.

Checking the List

We don't live in a giant, lifeless pond. We thrive and interact with others in a vibrant sea. If you're in a good place, it's time to give back. Pour your heart generously into others, and you will find that the current brings back a spirit of love to fill you again and again.

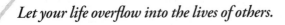 *Let your life overflow into the lives of others.*

Get Started

Sometimes you need to get your ducks in a row *before* you start.

Pilots need to go through their preflight checklist. Brain surgeons—after 20 years of schooling—need to get a good night's sleep, sync with their anesthesiologist and surgical team, study all the X-rays and scans, and prep every instrument that may be necessary to complete the operation. Dog walkers need to acquire several sturdy plastic bags before they head out the door.

But for many other tasks, it's not about preparation, it's about taking the first step. We put off joining a gym because we're not sure how all the machines work and we don't want to embarrass ourselves. Well, every member of that gym had a first day and understands that feeling.

We decide not to join a book club or small group because someone will say something that's really insightful and make us feel stupid. Well, in a room full of people there will always be individuals who know things and have thoughts you don't. But it's okay because you'll know things and have thoughts other people don't. Besides, that's why you join clubs and groups—to think and share new thoughts.

We're reluctant to try that new recipe because we're afraid our spouse will grimace. Well, as you serve the new dish, explain that you'd like their opinion but that grimacing is not acceptable. And then keep a heavy frying pan handy just in case.

When it comes to starting a family, today's newlyweds tend to delay. As a father of five who started young and cherished almost every moment, I encourage most couples not to wait until they're ready. If you're in love and optimistic for the future, then go for it. Being a parent is one of God's great gifts.

So what are you waiting to start? What item might God have written on your own personalized to-do list? Join a gym? Join a book club? Have a baby? Buy a home? College? Pottery classes? Open a diner? Secure an apprenticeship? Write your memoirs? Launch a podcast? Design your website? Mission work? Start a neighborhood Bible study? Learn a foreign language? Circle the globe? Learn Java? Develop a slider? Change careers? Build an ark? Patent your invention? Adopt a child? Jog? Blog? Get a dog? Eat a live frog?

You probably have something in mind already. You've been thinking about it and can envision yourself taking care of business, but you just don't know how to get started. Maybe that's why you picked up this book. To help clarify what God has next for you.

Well, if you need to do a little more research, then do that. If you need to get a license, passport, patent, or some other paperwork, apply this week. If you need a partner, ask that friend or acquaintance who's also eager to take a leap. But if you're waiting for a sign from God, that may not be as obvious as you hope.

Consider this. You've now read more than 50 chapters describing God's to-do list for your life. As you've turned each page, have you been scratching your head thinking, *This doesn't apply to me*? Or have you been breezing through, thinking some fresh thoughts, and confidently checking off just about every chapter?

Martin Luther King Jr. said, "You don't have to see the whole staircase; just take the first step."

A German proverb says, "Begin to weave, and God will give you the thread."

Benjamin Franklin said, "You may delay, but time will not."

And that's the best point of all. One year from now, you will either have gained a year's experience or will still be deciding whether or not to take the leap. In both cases, twelve months have gone by. Which means you can either spend the next year pursuing your dream, learning from mistakes, and getting ready for your second year of exploring life, or you can be waiting for someone else to take the glory. Glory you could have earned and given to God.

Checking the List

After that first step, fear subsides and the adventure begins.

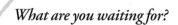 *What are you waiting for?*

Notes

1. Cited in A.P. Fitt, ed., *The Institute Tie*, volume 3 (September 1903 to August 1903), p. 122.

2. Art Rainer, "4 Dangers of a Leader's Echo Chamber" (blog post), December 23, 2015, http://www.artrainer.com/4-dangers-of-a-leaders-echo-chamber/.

3. R.C. Sproul, *The Prayer of the Lord* (Sanford, FL: Reformation Trust Publishing, 2009), cited in "A Simple Acrostic for Prayer: ACTS," *Ligonier Ministries*, February 10, 2014, http://www.ligonier.org/blog/simple-acrostic-prayer/.

4. "Number of available apps in the Apple App Store from July 2008 to January 2018," *Statista*, https://www.statista.com/statistics/263795/number-of-available-apps-in-the-apple-app-store/.

5. John Piper, "Embrace the Life God Has Given You," *desiringGod* (blog), March 10, 2017, http://www.desiringgod.org/embrace-the-life-god-has-given-you.

6. Peter Holley, "Stephen Hawking just moved up humanity's deadline for escaping Earth," *Washington Post*, May 5, 2017, https://www.washingtonpost.com/news/speaking-of-science/wp/2017/05/05/stephen-hawking-just-moved-up-humanitys-deadline-for-escaping-earth/?utm_term=.8060df35113a.

7. Tim Keller, "Questions for Sleepy and Nominal Christians," *Redeemer City to City* (blog), March 11, 2013, https://www.redeemercitytoity.com/blog/2013/3/11/questions-for-sleepy-and-nominal-christians.

8. Leah Marieann Kleet, "U2's Bono Shares the Biggest Thing He Learned About God and Himself After Reading the Psalms," *Gospel Herald*, May 10, 2017, http://www.gospelherald.com/articles/70412/20170510/bono-shares-biggest-thing-learned-god-himself-reading-psalms.htm.

9. "Stress Management," *Mayo Clinic*, http://www.mayoclinic.org/healthy-lifestyle/stress-management/in-depth/stress-relief/art-20044456?pg=2.

10. Jonathan Beber, "Want First Date Success? Share a Few Laughs," *eH Blog*, http://www.eharmony.com/blog/sharing-laugh-can-go-long-way/#.WTG4ivnytph.

11. Rhonda Byrne, *The Secret* (New York, NY: AtriaBooks, 2006), p. 9.

12. Robert Collier, *The Book of Life* (Jersey City, NJ: Start Publishing, 2012), cited in Byrne, *The Secret*, p. 49.

13. Victor Saad, "A Great Emcee" (blog post), May 3, 2017, http://victorsaad.com/a-great-emcee/.

14. John MacArthur, "Watching Your Spiritual Diet," *Grace to You* (blog), May 15, 2017, https://www.gty.org/library/blog/B170515.

About the Author

Jay Payleitner is one of the top freelance producers for Christian radio. For more than a decade, Jay produced *Josh McDowell Radio*, *Today's Father*, *Jesus Freaks Radio*, and *Project Angel Tree* with Chuck Colson.

Jay is a longtime affiliate with the National Center for Fathering and nationally known motivational speaker for Iron Sharpens Iron, marriage conferences, and even MOPS groups. Jay has sold more than a half million books, including the bestselling *52 Things Kids Need from a Dad* and *What If God Wrote Your Bucket List?* Jay's books have been translated into French, German, Spanish, Afrikaans, Indonesian, Slovenian, and Russian. He has been a guest multiple times on *The Harvest Show*, *100 Huntley Street*, and *Focus on the Family*.

Jay and his high school sweetheart, Rita, live in the Chicago area where they've raised five great kids and loved on ten foster babies. Jay and Rita are now celebrating the birth of grandchild number six!

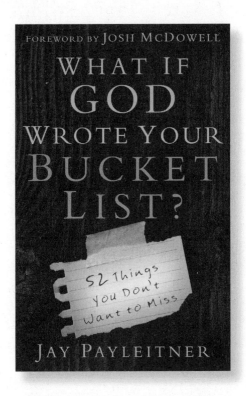

What If God Wrote Your Bucket List?

What's on your bucket list? If you checked off every item, would your life be complete? Maybe God has a better plan. Jay suggests 52 unexpected items for your bucket list to usher in purpose and joy today…and leave a legacy that just might make God smile.

More Great Harvest House Books by Jay Payleitner

52 Ways to Connect as a Couple
In these 52 short readings, popular author and speaker Jay Payleitner addresses head-on some of the obstacles to oneness and suggests out-of-the-box solutions for overcoming them. Sometimes spiritual, sometimes silly, but always practical, winsome, and wise, these ideas will help you connect and make your marriage better than ever.

52 Things Husbands Need from Their Wives
Jay digs deep to give practical, doable, fun, and unexpected ideas for a wife to connect with her husband by listening, remembering he's a man, encouraging him with her words, making space for him to participate, respecting him, and appreciating his "hero moments." Great steps for strengthening a marriage!

52 Things Wives Need from Their Husbands
For the husband who wants to live out God's plan for his marriage, *52 Things Wives Need from Their Husbands* provides a full year's worth of advice that will put you on the right track without making you feel guilty or criticizing you for acting like a man. A great gift or men's group resource.

It's Great Being a Dad
Jay joins veteran dads Brock Griffin and Carey Casey to offer their best practical advice so you can build awesome relationships with your kids. In partnership with the National Center for Fathering, these three men draw on their day-in, day-out experience to help you engage with daughters and sons in unexpected and life-affirming ways.

The Dad Book
Jay has packed this handy volume full of quick, inspiring help:

- fresh suggestions for engaging your kids
- dad-to-dad humor
- ways to show your kids instead of *tell* them
- encouragement and ideas to help your kids connect with God

Great confidence-booster for dads of any age and stage!

The Dad Manifesto
This pocket-size collection of tips, tricks, and tidbits provides the inspiration you need to become the best dad you can be. Each page features a fun project, a creative experience, or an important commitment that will help you establish a connection with your kids that will last a lifetime.

365 Ways to Say "I Love You" to Your Kids
You adore your kids, but expressions of love can get lost in the mayhem of daily living. Jay inspires you to show your affection, pride, and joy with 365 simple ideas that will encourage and nurture your child one loving moment at a time.

52 Things to Pray for Your Kids
How do you raise your kids up into godly young adults? Jay knows the power of sustained prayer over his children. With surprising insight into praying for your children's health, safety, and character, this resource will help you pray powerfully for *and with* children of any age.

10 Conversations Kids Need to Have with Their Dad
Straightforward, man-friendly advice about communicating all-important life values to your kids. Plant healthy thoughts about excellence, emotions, integrity, marriage, immortality, and five other key character qualities. A terrific, confidence-boosting resource for building lifelong positives into your family. Great gift or men's group selection.

52 Things Kids Need from a Dad
Straightforward features with step-up-to-the-mark challenges make this an empowering confidence builder with focused, doable ideas. Includes expanded insights on some of the rules in *The Dad Manifesto* and *no* long lists or criticism for acting like a man. Great gift or men's group resource! More than 150,000 sold.

52 Things Sons Need from Their Dads
These 52 quick-to-read chapters offer a bucketful of man-friendly ideas on building a father-son relationship. By your life and example, you can show your boy how to work hard and have fun, often at the same time; live with honesty and self-respect; and develop the inner confidence to live purposefully.

52 Things Daughters Need from Their Dads
Jay guides you into "girl land," offering ways to do things with your daughter, not just for her; lecture less and listen more; be alert for "hero moments"; and give your daughter a positive view of the male sex. You'll gain confidence in building lifelong positives into your daughter at every age.

The Little Book of Big Ideas for Dads and Daughters
This one-of-a-kind book features more than 50 fun and practical ways to build a great relationship with your daughter. Find out how you can make a difference in the most important parts of her life, such as her personal faith and relationships.

To learn more about Harvest House books and
to read sample chapters, visit our website:

www.harvesthousepublishers.com

HARVEST HOUSE PUBLISHERS
EUGENE, OREGON

What Is God Asking You "To-Do" Today?

When you talk to God about His plans for you, do you tend to focus on the far-off future? Big-picture thinking is great, but do miss out on what the Lord has in store for you today.

Inside, you'll encounter 52 unexpected action items, including.

- Make your bed. Achieve big things by starting small.
- Clear some clutter—out of your closet and your soul.
- Make the world wonder what got into you. And then tell 'em.
- Buy a used tuxedo. You never know when it might come in handy.
- Notice squirrels, armadillos, kangaroos…and God's glory in the world.

Don't wait! Pick a chapter, any chapter. God is calling you to be amazing right now!

Bestselling author and popular speaker **Jay Payle** as freelance radio producer for *Josh McDowell Rad* Voice of the Martyrs, and Bible League Interna include *52 Things Kids Need from a Dad, The Da What If God Wrote Your Bucket List?* Visit him at Ja

HARVEST HOUSE PUBLISHERS
HarvestHousePublishers.com